HOLLOWED
SOLDIER

Raped in the Military and Abandoned

ANNAMARIE IBRAHIM

BALBOA.PRESS
A DIVISION OF HAY HOUSE

Balboa Press books may be ordered through booksellers or by contacting:

Balboa Press
A Division of Hay House
1663 Liberty Drive
Bloomington, IN 47403
www.balboapress.com
844-682-1282

Print information available on the last page.

ISBN: 978-1-9822-5269-4 (sc)
ISBN: 978-1-9822-5271-7 (hc)
ISBN: 978-1-9822-5270-0 (e)

Library of Congress Control Number: 2020914701

Balboa Press rev. date: 08/20/2020

DEDICATION

To Aidar and Austin
"We will forever be...The Three Musketeers"

CONTENTS

PREFACE

With only a few exceptions, the blood running through my veins contains similar properties as other humans. Like you, my blood comprises mostly red cells, white cells, eosinophils, and a few other necessary ingredients. I've come to realize that I have one dominant cell compared to all the others. The other cell running through my body is a help cell. Although the help cell isn't an essential component of my blood, the desire and need to help someone improve their quality of life continually runs through my veins. The metamorphosis from an inspirational speaker for over three decades, to twice published author, best uses my help cells to fill in the hollowed parts that other people experience. These voids will fill again with joy, laughter, and love.

"*Hollowed Soldier*," is a direct result of my compulsion to use my life experience, primarily the violent and brutal rape I endured while serving in the US Air Force, to assist other women and men in overcoming similar experiences. I remained relatively silent for 35 years about the attack, rape, and wrongful discharge, while subsequently achieving a highly successful career as an inspirational speaker, trainer, and comedienne. During this success, my rape subject rarely came up as a point of discussion and was never discussed with an audience greater than two people.

The story details how, without provocation or expectation, Pandora's Box was cracked open, and the calculated conspiracy of my rape and abrupt discharge was exposed. Once presented with the opportunity to challenge the Veterans Administration's illegitimate decision and the wrongful discharge, I was poised to confront the good-old-boy testosterone-driven mentality of our military.

All of the characters, scenarios, and circumstances in this book are real. The motivational tools, techniques, and tips for developing an attitude of acceptance and perseverance are also quite real and well tested. It is with great pride that I share my footsteps to overcome and soar far beyond the hurdles and tragedies you may encounter.

Initially, the books *"Hollowed"* and *"Hollowed Soldier,"* were written under one title. In the middle of writing, the unexpected and tragic death of our only child at the young age of 32, devastated and hollowed my soul. My writing paused and my speaking ceased, while the tone of my inspirational teachings transitioned. Because I wanted to share the experiences and lessons derived from this tragedy, the original book grew too large for publication; it became necessary to spin-off the book *"Hollowed Soldier."*

The stories in each book are entirely different, and the emotional impact and benefits you'll discover in each one are unique. The principals I use to remain optimistic while fighting off pancreatic cancer, and live life with a hollowed body, are used to support my husband through cancer treatment for ALL. I share these techniques and more in the book, *"Hollowed - An Amazing True Story of a Woman Who Survived the Hollowing of Her Spirit, Body, and Soul."*

To receive the full benefit and fill your personal hollowed spirit, body, and soul, I highly recommend you read both books. Take time when you're reading to pause, reflect, and apply. Pause to digest the story and reflect on how it applies to your own life and the hardships you encounter. Take another moment to apply the changes you feel will help you grow and find joy in filling the hollowed parts of your spirit. It's best to use a highlighter to mark the moments in your reading that stir-up an emotion that gives you an "ah-ha."

It is with great sincerity that I say, "Thank you," for investing your time to read what I consider to be an inspirational seminar on paper.

CHAPTER 1

★ ★ ★ ★ ★

Boomerang – 2012

As a child, I was always fascinated by a boomerang. It was amazing how I could throw it out in the distance and it would circle back around for me to catch. As I've matured, I've discovered that if I'm not expecting it, a boomerang could also come back around to hurt me.

Θ   Θ   Θ

A twinge stings me directly in the center of my soul. It's similar to a pinch you feel as a dentist injects Novocain into the soft, sensitive tissue of your gums. This pinch doesn't take my breath away, but words can't describe how it burns. I've heard people refer to a twinge like this as female intuition or gut instinct. Regardless of the name you give it, I call it my inner voice, and right now it's screaming at me, *"Annamarie, watch out!"*

For decades this internal voice has been echoing in the bowels of my heart. I know this voice well; I'm an expert at dismissing and denying its existence. My husband, Aidar, is sitting in the

1

car downstairs; I hear him bellow out a call for me. "Annamarie, come on! Honey, it's time to go. Are you coming?"

We've been married for over thirty years, and he knows I don't typically run late. He may also suspect something is out of sync with me. I'm off-kilter and edgy. The engine of the car has been running the entire time he's been waiting. Exhaust fumes have built up like a thick fog of pesticide. I choke and cough when I finally enter the garage.

"Stop yelling! I'm here; I'm here. Let's go."

We haven't even moved twenty yards down our long driveway before Aidar puts on our brakes. Our son Austin pulls up in his car and parks. I love it when he surprises us and comes home unexpectedly; I feel as if our family puzzle is complete when we're all together. As an only child, Austin has participated in just about everything we do, but I didn't tell him we were headed out this morning. We call ourselves "the Three Musketeers"; we are indeed all for one and one for all, but it slipped my mind to let him know about this trivial opportunity.

He doesn't even close his car door before yelling, "Hey, where are you guys headed?"

"I'll explain later; we're late. We'll be back in a little while. Will you still be here?" I'm anxious to hear his response.

"Yeah, I need to do laundry; I'll be here for the weekend."

"Super. I love you. See you soon." I hope he never buys a washer and dryer; I like it when he comes home.

Located in the center of our busy town is a small community building. It's common practice for businesses and organizations to rent this room to host meetings and public events. Today the Solano County Department of Veterans Services is using this little facility to issue veterans cards to all of the local veterans. These cards are valuable; veterans will receive a 10 percent discount off their total purchase from a variety of local businesses. It's a win-win. The veterans win with some savings while the merchants gain publicity and increase the number of people shopping at their store. We've been remodeling our home; the savings we'll receive from stores like Home Depot and Lowes will come in handy.

The short trip in the car from our home to this community event is well worth the time, but the feeling gnawing inside me has expanded to impact my body's exterior. The little hairs on the back of my neck are beginning to shiver. In my right hand, I'm tightly holding my purse. The coloring of this purse will carry me through all the seasons of the year. It's dingy enough to accessorize with the dark-color outfits I wear during the winter months with just enough light touches to get me through the spring and summer. I don't like changing bags because I inevitably forget to transfer things I'll need. This bag has lots of pockets to hold the little stuff that comes in handy when you didn't even know you needed it. The critical part of this bag isn't the color or the pockets; it's what's inside, causing me to be nauseous. Smelling as if printed many lifetimes ago, a thirty-six-year-old document is tucked deep inside the pocket of this purse. The paper's fibers hold painful truths waiting to be released; just holding it makes my fingertips burn. The technical name for this document is "DD214." I've had mine folded into perfect thirds--, very perfect thirds. The size, condition, or quality of the paper doesn't determine its value; it's the words written on the page that make it unique. Codes and unknown numbers are written in tiny print and squeezed into small boxes on this form; only the people who speak military code are qualified to translate their meaning. I don't have to see what's written on this page to feel proud and be confident. This pride comes from the knowledge that my DD214 confirms I am an honorably discharged veteran of the USAF.

When we arrive at the center, I take the lead and walk up the pathway to the front door. No matter how hard I push on the door to enter the room, it won't open.

Aidar calls out, "Push it! Push harder!"

I snap back, "I am pushing!"

Leaning in with my shoulder, I put all my weight into one big push. Bang! Swinging open with much more force than I intended, the door flies open and slams into the doorstop mounted at the bottom. I'm embarrassed when this loud clang broadcasts my arrival. I don't like entering a room with such an announcement. Regardless of my embarrassment, my attention turns to the men sitting behind white plastic tables directly in front of me. Arranged in the shape of the letter L, two men sit at each table, surrounded by white paper stacks. I can't help but notice a few other gentlemen milling around. Surrounding the perimeter of this perfectly square room are metal folding chairs. Rubber feet cap the bottoms of the chairs to silence any noise they make when dragged across the floor. I suppose another purpose of the feet is to stop people from sliding when they sit down.

In the corner of the room stands a tall flag pole displaying the American flag. Proudly perched on the top of the pole is a large bronze eagle. The widespread wings and fierce-looking talons, give the impression its protecting the land and guarding the people. I'm honored and impressed with the sense of patriotism surrounding me. Directly in front of me are two men, veteran service officers (VSOs), with huge smiles. Decades have passed since I've been part of a military processing line; procedures haven't changed, and these men are the first step we need to take to receive this veterans' discount card.

As I pull out the copy of my DD214 wedged into my purse's pocket, the first friendly gentleman says, "Hello, thank you for your service to our country."

His voice is deep and daunting; I feel prompted by an old internal command telling me to stand at attention. Directly in the center of my throat, a lump begins to form; I can't seem to gather enough saliva in my mouth to push the lump down.

Softening the tone of his voice, "Ma'am? Ma'am? May I please have your DD214?"

"Oh, yes, I'm sorry. I have it right here for you." My voice is shaking almost as much as my hand.

"Yes, ma'am. Thank you, ma'am. May I also please see your driver's license?"

"My what?" I tip my head slightly, and my voice sounds very puzzled. I didn't anticipate him to ask for my driver's license; I'm just a little caught off guard and flustered. My fingertips feel numb, and I can't seem to make them work. There's an oval hole in the plastic covering that protects my license. By design, this hole is supposed to help remove the contents; mine isn't working. Fumbling to press my identification out from the thin plastic sheets, I sense he sees me shaking.

"Take your time, ma'am; I'm in no hurry." His voice is now calm and specific.

Doing my best to smile, "Thank you."

At last, my license breaks free of its protector. I hand it to him with my paperwork. He cuts a little fun into the conversation by holding my license up near my face to verify that I am who I say I am.

Smiling, he says, "Yep, yep, it's you all right."

I guess he approves because he passes my documents to the man sitting to his left and asks Aidar for his papers to determine his eligibility. The second man in this processing line reads through my papers and looks up at me and pauses. He looks up at me back and forth, and then he looks back down to the paperwork. My lips are beginning to feel heavy; the half-hearted smile on my face starts to dim. My thoughts are playing tricks on me. The sound of my heartbeat reverberates around my mind. Every shallow breath allows panic to settle into the empty spaces of my lungs that should be filling with air. I can only imagine the panic I feel in my heart can be seen on the look on my face. I just want out of this room.

Slam! A colossal noise resonates through the tiny room, and I jump. It sounds as if a gun went off; it echoes around the walls of the room. It doesn't seem as though anyone else was affected by the loud bang like me. In reality, my ears heard the sound of a metal stamp as it slammed down on my paperwork to mark it with the word *"approved"*, but my soul hears something much different. I hear the sound of my past swinging back to hit me on my head; it reaches down to tear at the core of my heart. I've only completed one table, and I'm shriveling up like a prune from the inside out. Feeling as if the entire room is draining of all oxygen, I think I'm beginning to wither, and my legs are getting weak. Standing at the point in the processing line where the corners of the two tables meet, I have a clue that I need to turn. Two more gentlemen sit smiling and ready to talk with me. Logically I know I'm fifty-five years old, but emotionally, I'm nineteen. If I weren't sure the year was 2012, I'd swear I was back in the Air Force, and the year is 1977.

The third man picks up my discharge papers, and like the two men before him, he reads them over thoroughly before talking to me. "Is there some mistake?"

My voice squeaks, "No, everything is fine."

An awkward pause in our conversation has emotionally made room for a colossal elephant to enter. It is gray and weighs approximately 15,000 lbs. I don't want to talk about this elephant, but it has decided to place its full weight on my chest. I can't breathe. People don't like to talk about the elephant in the room, and today is no different; this elephant is enormous.

Over and over again, I hear my inner voice begging for me to leave. More than ever, I wish I'd never come to this event. Like a giant boomerang, my past has come back around and struck me to the ground.

The gentleman who's holding my papers leans over to speak with the man sitting next to him. Although he's speaking in a whisper, I can't help but overhear him: "I think you'll want to take a look at this case; it doesn't make any sense."

He's right, it doesn't make sense, but it is still the truth. Tiny spots are floating in my vision, and it feels as though the community room is closing around me. I've almost finished the processing; only one man remains in the line. Tilting his glasses halfway down his nose, the last man I have to speak with is fumbling through my documents. In a whisper, he asks, "Is this right? Were you in the Air Force for only fourteen months?"

I manage to press out just enough air to speak, "Yes, that's right."

"You have a full and completely honorable discharge. Are you on disability?" His voice is calm, but the tipping of his head tells me that he's confused.

My entire body is numb, and I feel myself drifting farther away. Thankfully, Aidar reaches up to squeeze my left shoulder, and this touch brings my focus back to the conversation.

"No, no, I'm not on disability," I say. Despite my sense of panic, I feel a slight smirk come upon my face when this last man asks,

"Did you suffer a hearing loss while in the service?"

"No, I can hear you just fine." The look on my face tells him I think that was a stupid question.

"Did you ever apply to receive benefits for whatever injuries you did receive?"

I've never had poisonous gas pumped into my body, but the pressure I feel in my lungs right now is what I imagine it must feel like; I burn. My lungs feel as though they're on fire. This stranger just pushed the emotional trigger that made me feel light-headed and very dizzy; the room is spinning.

When a person is standing before a firing squad, a snare drum beats fast; I hear this beating now, but I don't see any drum. The beating sound is coming from the rapid beats of my heart as I begin to panic.

My senses are shutting down. I can barely hear what he's saying, but I read his lips to speak,

"I have the feeling there's more to this story. Were you ever turned down for disability? If so, is there something you'd like to tell me, or would you like to file another claim now?"

I think I know what's happening. I bet he's examined a lot of discharge documents where red flags jump off the page to capture his attention. He can quickly glance at my papers to see something is wrong. He's right! He can see a big piece of the puzzle missing. When he combines the information regarding the length of time I served in the Air Force, I received an honorable discharge and a new piece of information about not receiving disability. He knows something is wrong.

His eyes are kind; he sounds genuine. He has no idea he's just made a massive crack in Pandora's Box. I've tried my best to contain this horror for 35 years, but he's just let it out.

Holding his business card between his thumb and index finger, he extends his arm up for me to take the card from his hand. I can't move; it's my emotions that have caused me to feel frozen. Locked in a chamber of my mind are the memories from a time in my young life where I thought I was in a torture chamber from hell. Thoughts about this time are flashing at the front door of my conscious mind; they're knocking to come in. Aidar can see I'm not moving. I'm not taking this man's card, so he does it for me. Aidar takes the card and slips it into the side pocket of my purse. While still speaking to me, the gentleman looks Aidar directly in the eyes and says,

"If you'd like to come over and talk, I'll be in my office tomorrow. I think I may be able to help you. Sir, I'm not positive, but I believe your wife may greatly be able to help thousands of others. Thank you again for your service to our country."

My body feels frozen, yet my voice boils up and bursts out loud, "Thank you, I'll be fine. We'll be just fine."

The door to escape this room is only two feet away; I'm so close. As innocently as this man said his first comment, the gentleman who offered his card makes one last statement that pierces my heart.

"Again, I'm not positive about what may have happened to you, but YOUR voice may help those who aren't able to speak up for themselves."

This stupid ten-percent discount card drags me back over thirty-five years. I wonder what he means that "My voice may help others?" He doesn't know I'm a professional speaker; he doesn't know me.

The drive home was silent, Aidar never let go of my hand. Dinner tonight was routine, and here I now lay in bed, I can't sleep. Playing over and over in my mind like a broken record, the voice of the gentleman from the veterans' community event haunts me. I continually hear him saying, *"Thank you for your service to our country. Your voice can help those who aren't able to speak up for themselves."* He hit the nail on the head. I have a voice; I have the voice of a professional speaker. I had a voice when I was nineteen, but I didn't have the confidence and power that I now have. Plus, I didn't have anyone to help me.

Waking up exhausted, I'm also curious. I want to hear what the Veteran Service Officer from yesterday has to say. The only thing I'm sure of now is I'm no longer a frightened nineteen-year-old girl.

While I slip my shoes on to head out the door and to drive to the man's office, Aidar softly and lovingly whispers, "Would you like some company?"

Our eyes connect, and we hold our gaze for several moments, "Thank you, honey, but I want to handle this one on my own; I need to handle this on my own." The smile on his face feels extra loving when I tell him, "I'll probably need you close by when I come home."

His eyes are blinking extra fast; perhaps he's trying to hold back a few tears as he says, "I'll be right here for you."

Memories flood my thoughts while I drive to the VSO's office. These memories are of a rape I endured while in the service, and the thoughts are like a colorless, odorless, and lethal gas, capable of penetrating the corners of my mind. Just like the original rape itself, these memories are killing my ability to function normally. It's been over thirty-five years, and I'm constantly discovering areas of my life that have been greatly impacted by the rape. The impacts of these memories hide deep in the crevices of my character. Based on my behavior, no one else would see the damage to my psyche, yet it's nonetheless destructive.

My anger toward the man who raped me is equal to the rage and frustration I have toward the treatment I received from the "military justice system." I believed this system was there to support and protect me, not put a knife in my back and abandon me. My coping skills to get through life have, at times, been diminished by years of nightmares, feelings of self-doubt, and a lack of trust and self-respect. I've mastered the art of sculpting a fraudulent and deceptive exterior to appear confident and well-poised. I always look as though I'm very confident while I'm truthfully concealing a poor self-image. My coping techniques are often convoluted and misleading. I can teach others to improve their core beliefs about themselves while secretly working around this thorn in my heart. These coping techniques helped to make me a master of controlling my attitude, which has led to my success in business and relationships. When I think I've developed a skill to overcome challenging scenarios, a simple question thirty-five years later throws me back into active memory. Now I wonder if I've only been fooling myself.

Just as the smell of fresh-baked bread can take me back to the love in my grandmother's kitchen, the scent of a specific tube of lipstick takes me back to the night of my rape. My rapist used my lipstick to write on a mirror in my barracks. I know the smell; the smell reeks through my spirit. When I walk through a department store and pass through the cosmetic aisle, the scent of a specific brand of lipstick will yank me back to my night of hell. The tight binds from the scarves that held me to the bed during the rape are often brought to the forefront of my thoughts when a tight bracelet or watchband rubs me too tightly. When Austin was little, the playful game of Pin the Tail on the Donkey would trigger little moments of panic as the children cinched the blindfold around my eyes. I may not see any bruises on my ankles and wrists today, but I often feel the burn as I recall the night I struggled for hours to get loose. I wonder if I'll ever be free from the residue my rapist left behind. I've often questioned myself when I refer to the attacker as *"my"* rapist. It's almost as if I take ownership of him. He isn't *"my"* rapist; I don't own him, and yet I've let him become a part of me and not the other way around. I catch myself when I say that he *"is"* the rapist. I hate it when I give him power; I try to remember to refer to him as "was;" he "was" the man who raped me. A routine pelvic exam will bring me back to the processing of the rape kit in the emergency room. I still feel the sting and snap as pubic hairs were plucked from my body to compare with what the MPs gathered at the rape scene.

The question, "Are you sure?" reminds me of the constant badgering by the Military Police and Office of Special Investigations as they asked me, "Are you sure about your story? Now is the time to change it if you want to." I was hypersensitive and easily incensed for years following my discharge. The tension and nausea I feel when watching a violent scene on television are very real. I hate it when I see the sad expressions of Aidar and Austin as they observe me twisting the hair on my head to comfort myself. My sadness is very real, yet I try to hide my honest feelings of terror and hurt by masking it with a smile to put them at ease. Laid on top of the scars of the rape are other marks of pain. The look of pain and anger on the faces of my parents after speaking with them about my rape burns into my memory. The grimace my dad expressed as he learned of my rape details is as vivid today as when I witnessed it for the first time.

Thirty-five years. There isn't enough space to write down the ways the rape has impacted my life. It requires significant courage to simply take the trash out at night or walk alone in the dark. It's equally difficult to drive alone to a function or trust someone at their word. When I'm going to the same event as my friends, everyone knows that I don't like to carpool. I've been able to hide the reason for this behavior as a health issue. I tell everyone that in an emergency, I want to be able to leave quickly. The truth is, I'm afraid. The emergency I fear isn't always for my health; I fear I'll be hurt or confined. I need to know that if I want to leave, I can. Three or four of my friends will get in a car together, and everyone is comfortable and understanding with me driving in my car behind them; everyone understands.

The drive to the Solano County Department of Veterans Services is long and slow; I think I can feel each rotation of the tires on the car. If this were a movie, the camera would be focusing on the slow turning of the odometer; the music playing in the background would be tense and dark. We'd feel the drawn-out tones of the bass with the deep stroking sounds of its bow as it was being dragged across the strings to exemplify my apprehension. Music is the best reference I have at this time to describe my emotions; words can't come close. I can't say I hold the anger in my heart because that's where I keep my love, but I'll confess I do have anger. Despite being a motivational and inspirational speaker who's gifted with the skills to convince others they can overcome anything, I struggle myself to overcome the feelings of anger I have over the rape. I'm comfortable talking with my family and select friends about the details of my rape and wrongful discharge, but I've yet to stand on stage and share my story with an audience. Maybe, this Veteran Service Officer will present me with an opportunity where I might be able to take my first step to speak about it and share my story. First, I need to find a way to trust him.

I don't have any documentation with me today. I'm comfortable without it. Deep within me is the confidence of the truth; this is all the documentation I need. This truth holds me as strong today as it did in 1977. Nothing this man can say or tear open inside of me will change the facts.

When I finally arrive at the reception desk, I see a clipboard with a sign-in sheet wedged tightly beneath a metal clip. I need to fill in the name of the person I'm here to see. I guess it's time to look at the name on the business card. In my attempt to depersonalize this experience, I have only looked at the address on the card he gave me. I haven't wanted to make a human connection. I see on the card that I'm here to see a man named Tom.

Deep breaths calm my nerves, and I now find myself sitting across the desk from Tom. It's difficult to believe that it was only yesterday when he saw through the discrepancy of my documents. I believe it was the look on my face that prompted him to ask further questions and uncover a ghost. Depending on what he has to say to me, I pray this ghost is excised from my core.

This time I'm taking control; I will set the tone of this meeting.

"Sir, please don't take this personally. I honor and value our armed forces. I respect and appreciate everything they do to defend and protect our country. I'm a patriotic and loyal person, but let me be honest with you. I don't trust any veterans group or, for that matter, any group affiliated with the military. Right now, that's how I see you."

Tom sighs and lays down the pencil he's been rolling around with his fingers. Slowly and with specific intent, he leans forward with his hands clasped. It looks as if he's about to pray when he says,

"I respect your position. I don't know anything about your situation, but I'm glad you came in to see me today. I told a few members of my staff about you this morning. I don't know what or why; I'm just glad you're here. Thank you for coming. If it's alright with you, may I share a few facts with you and ask you a few questions?"

For the moment, I'll let Tom take the lead in our conversation; he's respectful. Tom is cautious in his manner of speech; his questions are sensitive yet probative; I think he suspects what may have happened. One by one, I answer his questions and slowly reveal the events leading up to my wrongful discharge. His eyes tear up while I share my story; it's not easy for me either. He drastically changes his body posture as I share my experience of the attack, the rape, and the lack of support. His shoulders soften with empathy, tense up with anger, and lock with frustration. The way he's nodding his head and rubbing his hair lets me know he's paying attention to what I'm saying. I feel he recognizes I'm a wounded veteran, a doubtful person, a damaged woman. Most importantly, I think he understands. I feel his compassion washing over me. Although my specific circumstances may differ from others, he sadly informs me of similar cases with other servicemen.

I can hear the frustrated tone in his voice when he asks, "Why didn't you file a claim with the Veterans Administration (VA) when you were first discharged? They could have supported you. You should have received medical benefits, assistance with going to college, and many more services to help you."

Instantly I feel the anger and sadness swirl up inside of me. The tone of my voice changes when I respond, "I did! I did file a claim! Without so much as a single exam, they denied my claim."

He has a slightly confused look on his face when he asks, "Why didn't you file an appeal?"

"I was only nineteen years old. I was traumatized, humiliated, confused, and angry. I just wanted it all to be behind me. It was 1977; the support for raped women didn't exist. There was no such thing as the diagnosis of Post-Traumatic Stress Disorder

(PTSD). There was certainly no description to be associated with Military Sexual Trauma (MST). My parents were of the old belief that you don't air your dirty laundry. Their philosophy was to be grateful you're alive; grateful you didn't get pregnant."

Tom jumps up, "We need to file an appeal. This is wrong; this year alone, there have been over 20,000 service members sexually assaulted. All too often, the victims are assaulted twice, and with your strong voice, I know that you can help others to speak up and stop this horrible practice that's far too common in our military."

"Please," I ask, "Give me a moment."

Suddenly an inner voice cries out. *"Annamarie, you're not alone. Aidar is with you no matter what. Trust this man Tom."* Taking on the big machine of the military justice system or the Veterans Administration is a big deal.

The memory of walking onto Lackland Air Force Base for the very first time pops into my mind. I was in San Antonio, Texas, to attend basic training. It was hot and humid, nothing like California. It was necessary to remove our sense of individuality by stripping us down of our civilian clothes. Uniforms were issued to us to remove our freedom of independent expression and build our outward appearance of unity. The only independent feature we were allowed to maintain was the length of our hair, and even that had to be put up into a cap and not allowed to touch our collar. I recall walking down the sides of the flight line, where the airplanes landed searching for cigarette butts. It was a strange exercise because we were forbidden from smoking anywhere near the flight line. How could there be cigarette butts when there was no possibility of cigarettes? Trained to follow orders, we knew better than to question why; it was a necessary mind game. When one person in our squadron made a mistake while trying to march in line and perfect sequence, we were all punished. This punishment was to walk for hours until we mastered the march; this included walking in the rain or heat. When exercising and performing calisthenics, if one airman wasn't in perfect form, we all had to do an additional hundred sit-ups. The importance of developing as an airman who respects and fears their superior officers is what I learned. I'm still in support of the importance of this training for our military. We can't have individuals second-guessing the decisions of their superiors, especially in the event of war. We all knew to relinquish our opinions and trust our upper command respectfully. From day one, I never doubted that my fellow airmen and the upper command would have my back whenever needed.

After basic training, I received orders to report to Chanute Air Force Base in Rantoul, Illinois, where I received my technical training. The cold winter of Illinois followed the hot summer in Texas. I've never lived in such a cold place. My bones felt like frozen sticks of chalk that were fragile, crisp, and painful. It was an unusually cold and harsh winter with record-setting winds bringing the icy cold temperatures deeper into my pores. Whenever we went outside, those fierce winds made it necessary to wear face masks to protect us from frostbite. I enjoyed being a part of the Air Force; the chill of the wind or the sun's heat never impacted my loyalty. Upon graduating from technical school in the field of Life Support, I was excited to receive my orders to a duty station in Southern California. My next duty station was George Air Force Base in Victorville, California, smack dab in the middle of the desert. I was assigned to work in the parachute shop, where I packed a variety of parachutes and worked on life support equipment. Some of the chutes I was responsible for packing stopped a plane while landing on the runway; these were drogue chutes. I recall packing many different types of chutes, including chutes attached to the pilot's ejection seat. When a pilot ejected from a plane in high altitude, these chutes open automatically. In high altitude, the oxygen is too low, and the pilot could be unconscious; the chute needs to open on its own. Every parachute rigger is required to sign off and take responsibility for the proper packing of the chutes they pack. After completing technical school, there's still a probation period before certified or proficient parachute rigger. A Technical Training Instructor was required to co-sign on every chute I packed until I certified on the various types of chutes. It was going to take another year of specific training on parachutes at George Air Force Base to be able to sign off on my work independently.

Early one morning, I recall seeing someone from Quality Control walk into the parachute shop. Hearing my name mentioned in the conversation, I concentrated closely to overhear what they were saying. I was shocked. Before taking off on a test flight, a pilot checked the riser attachment on the chute for his ejection seat and noticed a problem. One of the risers had a slight twist that could have caused a problem if he needed to deploy the chute in an emergency. The Quality Control Officer was there to notify me of the twist, but it was my Technical Training Instructor who received the citation. My Training Instructor was responsible for checking my work; he was responsible for the error. Shit may flow downhill, but accountability is the responsibility of the entire unit. Witnessing firsthand the importance of working as a single unit, and to always work as a team is awesome. Moments like this made me appreciate the psychological games and practices established in the basic training at Lackland Air Force Base. It's through the stripping down of the ego that helps to build the unit and unify the squadron. Ordered to make our beds and stand beside them for inspection was a regular practice in basic training. The First-Sargent would walk past our bunks, and I could smell the fear of my entire unit. Hearts were pounding as the First-Sargent walked up to each of our bunks to inspect them and our uniforms. Regardless of how perfectly each of us had made our bunks, we'd hear him shout, "This is perfect! Now, do it again!" He ripped down the covers while simultaneously tearing down our egos.

Running through the confidence course comprised of rope swings hanging over pits of mud, tall walls to scale over, and repel down. We also had many other physical activities to condition our agility and strength. All of us understood until the last member of our team had made it through successfully—we weren't finished. We dedicated our energies to the airman who needed assistance. Every thought in my head and heart was to our country. I was a loyal and trustworthy soldier.

Regardless of my loyalty and dedication, it was the rapist who stripped me naked and left me damaged and bound to a bed. Despite my unwavering respect and admiration, it was my upper command that didn't have my back. It was the huge red, white, and blue machine that deserted and discarded me out to the civilian world without support or consideration. For decades I've been haunted by the unwillingness of my upper command to hold the rapist accountable. I have struggled with their hypocrisy of not standing by their principles of protecting their team members and fellow soldiers. Today, the thought of confronting this machine is intimidating, but I'm fully prepared to take it on; I can do this.

The energy from these memories bubbles up within me, and I feel energized. Before I walk out of the office, Tom is pleased when I tell him I'm going to do it. I'm going to file an appeal. Giving me a big hug and sending me off with my first assignment, he thanks me for trusting him. I confess I'm feeling very skeptical when I say, "We'll see."

Aidar must have heard my car coming up the road to our home because he's already standing out front to greet me. "Well, how are you doing?"

Confidently I share, "I'm fine. I need you. I want to take on the VA and fight to appeal the decision they made in 1977."

Annamarie at Lackland AFB, Texas

CHAPTER 2

★ ★ ★ ★ ★

Revealed

As parents, it's challenging to teach our children to be confident enough to ask someone they don't know for help while also teaching them to be leery of strangers. Teaching a child to be skeptical is crucial for their survival. One of the most challenging lessons to teach is to know who they can trust.

Weeks have passed since I filed my first paperwork to obtain copies of my military medical records. I never knew it would be so difficult. One notice after another comes in the mail stating I need to apply to a different facility. Two steps forward and one step back; make a right turn; left turn; I can't move on. If anyone thinks I'll become frustrated and give up, they've thoroughly misjudged me. The nineteen-year-old girl who was left drained of all her confidence has developed into a woman who is relentless in her older age. I'm suspicious my records have mysteriously disappeared.

Six months have passed; I'm only slightly tired and a tad bit disheartened. As I look inward at my true feelings and not the emotions I express on my face, *disappointed* isn't the best word to describe what I'm feeling; I'm getting angry! I'm going to use this anger to do something constructive, so I move forward by contacting my congressman. It's amazing how the political pressure of a respected official will produce documents long thought to be missing. One phone call from a staff member from my congressman's office and my medical records magically appear in my mailbox. From now on, I'll always think of our congressman as "my magician."

The stack of forms the VA requires to appeal for disability benefits is daunting, yet I'm not discouraged. I'm baffled at the redundancy of the questions, but it's the occasional feeling of suffocation that stirs up emotions in my heart. These emotions move up from my heart into my throat; this is when I feel suffocated. It's not the paperwork that's the problem; it's the memories. I'd prefer to run away from this terrifying section of memory lane, not stroll down and replay it.

The VA requires documentation from every doctor I've seen since my discharge in 1977. With my extensive history of health challenges, this research is daunting. I'm developing a newfound respect for medical transcriptions while I collect these files. Some notes are impossible to read. The handwriting of doctors is like chicken scratch. No matter how exasperated I become with the process, the congressman's team stays involved in my progress providing encouragement and support. The congressman's staff frequently contacts the VA to double-check their receipt of documents and clarify conversations. Tom and his team at the Solano County Department of Veterans Services quickly help me with every necessary form. When my mailbox becomes stuffed full with notices from the VA claiming I was remiss in filing an essential document, Tom and his team jump right in to back me up with proof of delivery. The larger struggle for me is the battle I'm having with the memories of my rape. One moment I'm confident I can continue with this appeal, and the next, I'm full of fear and doubt; my resolve is melting like sugar in water. I understand why Aidar and Austin tiptoe around the subject of my appeal; they never know how to react. To regain my resolve, I need to get angry again.

Making myself comfortable to examine all the documents, I sit on the floor of my office and press my back up against the wall. Through the thin fabric of my shirt, I feel the spackle's uneven texture spread heavily on the Sheetrock. Like a hawk, I carefully scan each document. The first document to catch my eye is another DD214. It looks very similar to the one I received with my separation, but this one has additional discharge codes. No one should ever have two DD214s. Something's wrong---very wrong.

The average person didn't have a personal computer in 1977. Google wasn't a household word like it is today. Even when I did have my first computer, I'd never have thought to pull up my discharge papers. Even if I had a computer, it couldn't explain why my original DD214 had different codes that the one I just found in their files.

I pull myself up off the floor to sit in front of my computer, and type in the letters for the new codes I've discovered. It's incredible how fast Google pulls up the information to identify the code SPN: HMB. The codes on this second document state I received a discharge because I have a "character of behavior disorder."

I'm stunned. I haven't a clue what "disorder" I supposedly had before enlisting in the air force. I'm confused and appalled at this reference because I had no indication of a "character of behavior disorder" for the previous nineteen years. I had no disorder when I was promoted a few months before the rape. It worked; I'm angry. No, I'm beyond angry. I'm furious. Both DD214 forms state I received an honorable discharge. I didn't receive a general discharge, medical discharge, or dishonorable discharge. Mine was honorable, and I've received many VA loans on our homes because of this.

The floor above me is creaking; it must be Aidar walking around in the kitchen. While ripping open another manila envelope containing more documents, I yell to him at the top of my lungs.

"Aidar, Aidar, come here. I'm so pissed." My hands are shaking uncontrollably.

I can hear the panicked tone in his voice as he comes running down the stairs shouting,

"What's wrong? What's wrong?"

Shaking the newly discovered DD214 in the air, I shout, "Look at this. They claim I had a character of behavior disorder. How can they say that? They don't want to admit that I was on the base when I was raped."

My hands are trembling as I take out another document. "Look at this one too. Look! Look! Here's another document that goes on further to claim I've had the disorder since birth. How can they lie and say I had a disorder since birth? What disorder? This is absurd. If I had a disorder, why did they accept me into the service in the first place? How was I able to get through high school without any issues? How was I able to go to college without any problems? How could I never have had an incident at any previous time in my life if I had a disorder? How is it I never spoke to a psychologist or counselor before in my life, not even a school counselor? Up until the point I was raped, I had never seen a psychologist or psychiatrist, *ever*! A *disorder*? What the heck!"

Sliding off of the chair to sink back into the floor and the mound of documents, I crawl over to the metal file cabinet and lean my back up against the cold steel. My knees are pressed tightly against my chest and Aidar is close by my side. With his hand resting firmly on my knee, together, we examine each document. I'm so grateful he's here with me; he's the solid rock

I need to stay grounded. Every page and report takes me down a painfully long road to a living hell I thought I'd escaped.

My emotions are different than I expected. I'm sad as well as angry, and I have an equal amount of disgust. I'm beyond angry to discover someone has intentionally inserted the word "possible" in the margins outside the word "rape"; I'm outraged. The emergency-room physician has documented rape, but the word "possible" now sits in the margins with two squiggle lines beneath it to draw attention. Arrows from the word "possible" are drawn over to the word "rape" to identify where it should be inserted.

"Oh, my God! Honey, look at this." I hand the papers over to Aidar, "Whoever wrote the word "possible" in the margins after the report was complete, didn't even attempt to copy the writing style of the doctor who originally wrote the report. Look, they didn't even use the same ink pen."

The well-documented medical records indicating my hospital stay and treatment for rape, contradict any attempt the military has made to alter the facts. I arrived at the emergency room, where they admitted me into the hospital for three days; it's documented here in the report. Within the medical record, there are many notations of the bruises and lacerations on my wrists and ankles. The medical reports document the treatment I received for a rape, any additional words or comments written after the fact in the margin can't erase the facts of record. Overshadowing the attempt to hide evidence of my rape is a document stating, "A further study by the Office of Special Investigation (OSI) is warranted." All of this has lit a fire in me. I'm angry in a good way.

Tom and his team at the Veterans Assistance Office are incredibly supportive. Additionally, the office of my congressman is a lethal tool I grasp tightly in my hand. I'm not holding my support team like a pencil; I embrace them like a dagger. My appeal package is thick, but it's heavily laden with emotional and factual words and phrases.

One-hundred-twenty-five steps! I've counted the number

of steps I take each day to walk down our steep driveway to our mailbox. It's another one hundred twenty-five steps back up the hill too. Multiply this by six days a week and I'm up to six thousand steps a month. Multiply this by the eleven months I've been waiting for news, and I figure I've taken over sixty-six thousand steps to pick up a letter. When I walk down the driveway, I'm always full of hope. Walking back up the driveway, empty-handed has become far more difficult. It's not my thighs that burn; it's my attitude. Occasionally I'll receive a letter, and I stand beside the mailbox to rip it open. I'm now personal friends with our mailman Ramon. I'm becoming experienced at using the weight of a letter to predict its contents. A lightweight envelope is usually a notice to state my request is still under review. A two-page letter has a little more weight. The VA uses two papers to notify me they need additional information or need me to complete a different form. Most of the time, I've already supplied the information they request, but now they need it filled out on a document with a different number; the same information and various forms. The staff in my congressman's office continues to come to my aid. On a few occasions now, my congressman's team has challenged the VA's claim that I wasn't within the allotted time to provide information. I'm extra vigilant to "cross a T or dot the letter I." I'm also careful to maintain two copies of every piece of information I have ever provided, and the mail is always sent by certified mail; I have a signature to prove it arrived. The VA has a website where a veteran can establish an account to check the progress of their claim; I've done this. I check the site every day, yet the progress shows a big fat nothing.

Like every other day, I lock my feet into the groove I've blazed while walking down the hill to pick up Ramon's mail. The path I've worn resembles the line cut in the grass by cattle walking to food. Day after day, the cows cut down the grasses as they walk; they make a groove; a rut. My assumptions about the weight of an envelope and its contents might be wrong. I've caught Ramon before he has the opportunity to stuff the mail into the box, so he hands it to me personally. The envelope is still light, but this time the VA informs me they've scheduled me a meeting with an independent investigative psychiatrist. My appointment will last approximately sixty-minutes, and I must bring Aidar along with me.

I was only called to the principal's office once as a girl, seeing the psychiatrist feels similar. My knee jerk reaction is to panic. How will this person examine my thoughts and manipulate my head? Beginning a few years after my rape, I've seen plenty of psychiatrists and psychologists. Rationally I understand they're "supposed" to be neutral and objective; but, this is the VA who is making the request, and I'm suspicious. My paranoid thoughts have me suspecting otherwise. I'm also concerned about why they want Aidar to come with me. He wasn't there in 1977, what can he add to the conversation?

The day of the appointment has finally arrived. The only calm thing is the air; it's certainly not me. On the outside, I appear tranquil and at peace with what's about to happen. Aidar knows the truth.

On the morning of our scheduled psychiatric interview, I've styled my hair in a mature, confident manner, and my make-up is tidy. Looks are very deceiving; my stomach is in a knot and floating with extra acid. The first fifteen minutes of our drive is quite. Not much conversation is taking place, so I decided to break the ice and ask, "What do you think will happen in this exam?"

"Honey, you've asked me this same question a dozen times. Just tell the truth and be yourself."

My nerves bring out the sarcasm in me, "Truth? Really? You want me to tell them the truth? When did telling the truth about what happened ever help me in the past? Of course, I'll tell the truth. It's the truth that's on my side, but I still don't trust them."

Aidar wears the scars of my sarcasm. He's learned it's best to keep quiet when this side of my personality appears. The rest of the drive to San Francisco is quiet. I look out the window as we fly past the cars; Aidar has a heavy foot and enjoys driving fast. San Francisco is notorious for not having great parking. I'm surprised how quickly we find a space; minutes of free parking remains on the meter. It must be our lucky day. The instant we walk into the psychiatrist's office, I can't help notice the bad lighting in the room. A fluorescent light flickers on and off; it makes me blink, and the buzzing sound coming from the light bulbs sets my nerves on fire. The smell is damp and musty; it looks like they just shampooed the carpet. Two large box-fans sit at the end of the long haul and directly blow the stale air. There's no way to get around the fans; they block the entrance to the office door.

"Boy, it stinks in here. Don't you think it stinks?" I ask.

"No, I don't think it's too bad. It's just an old building, and you're nervous."

"The fact that I'm nervous has nothing to do with the fact it stinks!"

My temperament is tightly wound, and it's precisely at moments like this that I'm incredibly grateful for Aidar's patience with me. He just smiles and reaches for the doorknob to open the door. He knows I'm nervous. The chipped paint on the door leading into the doctor's office is noticeable; the scratched brass doorknob has evidence of many years of twists and turns. A receptionist greets us with an offering of coffee, but I think I'm jacked up enough. We say thank you and take a seat on the green couch pressed up tightly against the wall.

My interview is first; they request Aidar to remain in the lobby. I feel bad that he has to be stuck trying to read with the light going on and off like a twitching nerve in the corner of a tired eye. Before I head into the doctor's office, I squeeze his arm and softly plant a quick kiss on his cheek. In return, I receive a slight smile and a wink. "You've got this baby. I'll be right here for you when you're all done."

Two comfortable chairs sit in front of her desk, and I've decided to take the one on the right. The neatly organized papers on the top of her desk and the large laptop computer in the center of her desk, lead me to believe she's ready to begin. Talk about the traffic, weather, and the easy parking in front of her office quickly conclude. Without hesitation, she opens up the conversation,

"I want to assure you I'm an independent psychiatrist hired to review your claim and investigate the facts. I'm not an employee of the Veterans Administration. My practice is private, and the VA has arbitrarily hired me to conduct this investigation and submit my findings in a report."

The doctor begins to ask her questions; I find them similar to the ones you'd find in a career assistance class in college. The same questions come up again and again, but she phrases them differently each time she asks; I think she's looking for inconsistencies. We talk about marriage, children, and "life" in general. Our conversation is moving right along until she asks the big one:

"Please tell me in as much detail as possible about the events leading up to your discharge. Specifically, please tell me about the rape."

I take a big breath and lean forward in my chair, "I was stationed at George AFB in Victorville, California, working in the Parachute Shop; it's also called Life Support. Do you know what Life Support is?"

"No, but that's okay, please go on."

"Well, some parachutes are extremely heavy. Because I was lifting them so often, I was continually injuring my back. The drag chutes are especially heavy; they're the chutes they use to stop the planes. After many visits to the doctor with strains and injuries, the doctors requested I be re-trained for another job. Finally, I received notice that the request was approved. I was excited. I was able to stay in the Air Force, and I wasn't going to hurt my back any further. I shared the news with everyone I knew. I think I shared the news with anyone who would listen. At the time, I enjoyed writing poetry; it was a creative way to express my thoughts and feelings. I'd write poems and daily journals in a spiral-bound notebook; it was nothing fancy. It was in the early evening, and I decided to take the short walk from my barracks to the large community center where I liked to sit and write. I went to the large community room because I wanted a change of scenery from my tiny bedroom. I think I was only there for one or two hours when I decided to walk back home; I didn't want to be out when it was super dark. There was a large open space between the center and my barracks; it wasn't a park; it was just an open space. There were some tall trees in this space; no grass; just dirt. I didn't see it coming, I didn't see anyone near me, but suddenly, someone grabbed me and pulled me into a dark area below the trees. When I finally understood what was happening, I realized it was a man. I was wearing my green fatigues, not my casual civilian clothes. He pulled me down to the dirt from the back of my shirt; he grabbed my collar. I kicked and screamed as loud as I could. I mean, I kicked hard and screamed at the top of my lungs. My head hurt when he pushed it against the trunk of one of the trees. Why I remember the tree so clearly doesn't make much sense to me, but I do. I mean, it's been thirty-five years now, and I still remember the bark and dirt. Some details are as clear as the skin on the back of my hands; other memories tucked into places in my memory, jump out when I least expect. Bark and dirt….I tasted bark and dirt."

It's all I can do to hold back my tears. My lips are quivering. No matter how hard I blink to keep tears from rolling down my face, I can't stop them. Sharing specific details of my rape makes me emotional; today is no different. The one thing that's different about today is from where I'm deriving my motivation. Today, talking with this psychiatrist, I find comfort in the hope that I'll be helping others. Sadly, I know rape will happen to far too many people in the military. Not only will they be raped, but they'll receive a wrongful discharge. Like me, others will ask for help, but they'll get denied.

Anger begins to fuel my confidence; I'm empowered to continue telling her about my experience. I hope the VA will eventually see how many decades the military has permitted rape to continue and do something about it. I'm not alone; there are thousands like me. My experience dates back to 1977. Rape and wrongful discharge have continued without punishment long before me. There are way too many victims who haven't yet found the power to speak out. I can't quit now; I have to stay with the fight.

Pulling out a box of Kleenex, she asks, "Would you like a tissue?"

"Yes, maybe, I would. Thank you."

Filling my lungs with a big breath of air, I boldly pick up where I left off.

"My screams scared him. He pushed me face down in the dirt and ran away. I've always wanted to believe he ran away because he realized I was stronger than he anticipated. Who knows; I guess we'll never know. He ran away, but he picked up my book of poems and took them with him. I never saw his face. I ran to the closest barracks, beat on a door, and screamed for help. It was only a few minutes before the Military Police (MP) arrived and took a report of the incident. A few hours later, I was escorted to my barracks and left to go on about my life. The MPs said they thought it was a one-time thing; I had no reason to think otherwise. I convinced myself it was some strange guy who seriously had a problem. I'd always felt safe on the base. I had every confidence in the police when they said they'd make a full investigation. Yes, I was scared and upset about what had happened, but again, I had no doubt someone was going to investigate it. It was over; I thought it was over. I wasn't afraid to go back to my barracks; many women lived there. I think there were a total of 40 women between up-stairs and down. I was sad he took my poems, but I wasn't afraid to be back in my room."

Before Aidar and I walked into her office this morning, I didn't think I was going to say too much. When I discovered the DD214 claiming I had a "character of behavior disorder," I was afraid she would twist my words. I thought the psychiatrist would contort what I said to fit the code. Now that I'm here and I've started talking, she's making me feel comfortable; now I won't shut-up. I'm not going to be quiet. I'm going to use this forum to tell my story. I have an audience, and I'm not letting her go until she hears it all.

The cuff of my shirt sleeve is too long; I feel it rolling in the palm of my right hand. While I've been talking, I've been moving it around with my fingertips. The texture of the material is bumpy and rigid; I find comfort in fidgeting with it. I know the conclusion to this story, and I'm already feeling anxious. I haven't even begun to share the most intricate details.

"Please continue and tell me what happened next."

"Next?" My thoughts are drifting. "Yes, what happened next? Well, following the attack, I went to work as usual. My neck was red from having my shirt yanked, but I was fine enough to go in. I told the men at my shop about the attack. Everyone offered to walk with me wherever I needed to go, but I was fine. A few days later, I don't remember exactly how many days had passed, but it was just a few. I was asleep, and something woke me up. I think it was a noise; I don't know for sure. Since I was awake, I thought I might get up and go down the hall to the bathroom. I've thought about this a million times. In hindsight, I know this was when I made my mistake; I sure didn't know it then."

The psychiatrist pushes her chair back a little farther from her desk and crosses her legs.

"Please go on."

"My room was the first bedroom off of the community day room. Only a door separated the day room from the hall. There was a bathroom in the very center of the barracks with rooms on either side. Everyone shared one bathroom in the middle of each floor. There was only one phone for each floor, and that was right across from the bathroom. I remember I walked past a girl who was up late talking on the telephone. I waved at her before I walked inside. When I finished in the bathroom, I walked back down the hall to my room. My bedroom door was open a little bit, just the way I left it. I remember something being a little strange because I heard music. I still didn't think anything of it. I thought the music was coming from the community dayroom; it couldn't come from my room. The barracks were old, the walls were paper-thin, and people regularly gathered in the dayroom. Because many people worked night-shift or split-shift, it wasn't uncommon to hear music playing at all hours of the day. I opened the door to my room and walked inside; it was pitch-black; it was just how I left it. I remember being confused because the music wasn't coming from the day room; it came from 'my' room. For some reason, my little stereo was playing music."

Pausing for a moment, I take a big breath and run my fingers through my hair.

"Would you like a glass of water?" she asks.

"Yes, please. That would be nice."

After I drink some water, I feel better. My voice is a little louder.

"I wasn't alone. When I walked back into my room, I wasn't alone. Somebody was in there. Whoever it was must have come in when I was in the bathroom. My room was so dark; I never saw who it was. He grabbed me from behind and used his hand to cover my mouth. It was a man, and he said he had a knife. He told me that if I screamed, he'd hurt me; actually, he said he'd cut me. He tied something around my mouth. I later learned it was one of my scarves. I've always liked scarves, and he used one of my scarves. I was afraid of being cut; even worse, I was afraid he would kill me. It was that fear that kept me quiet. With another scarf, he covered my eyes and tied it around my head. Pushing me down on my bed, he used another scarf to tie me to the bed. He tied my arms first and then my legs. You see, the bed was metal, and he used the metal legs to tie me down. I remember asking myself, 'Who is this? Why are they doing this?' Don't ask me how many times he raped me, I don't remember. I don't know how many hours I was there either. One thing I do remember; I remember feeling like I was drowning."

I pause for a moment, and she asks, "Are you alright?"

"Yes. I'll be fine. I just need a moment."

"Take your time."

"You see....When I was young, my parents taught me how to swim. I never learned what to do when being raped. That's just not something we teach our kids. We teach our children how to swim underwater. We teach them to hold their breath and kick. I couldn't kick, he had me tied down. A baby knows by instinct to hold their breath underwater. There's no instinct for rape. A woman doesn't know what to do. So while he raped me, I disappeared. I went somewhere in my head where no one could hurt me. I went to a place in my head that had walls. In my safe place, no one could come in or out. I was safe here. When he climbed off me, I heard him whispering. He was reading my poems to me, my very own poems. When I came out of the safe place in my head and concentrated on what he was saying, I realized who he was. It was him; the guy who attacked me underneath the trees a few nights before."

"How did it make you feel when he was reading your poems?"

"Feel? I don't know that I was able to feel anything. Occasionally I'd come up from the private place in my thoughts to listen if he was still there. I was so scared, but I was equally confused. I was so confused I didn't even initially make the connection to what happened a few nights before. I knew I couldn't escape, so I didn't try. If I didn't feel him touching me, I'd listen and try to hear his breathing. So, to answer your question, I was doing my best not to feel anything. I do remember wondering what I did wrong to deserve being tied to my bed and raped."

She has a curious look on her face and asks, "What made you think you'd done something wrong?"

"That's what I couldn't figure out. It took me years to understand that I didn't do anything wrong. But again, at that time, I was only nineteen. To this day, I'm a people pleaser. I can look back now and see why I felt this way. But at that time, I couldn't see it. I laid there thinking I'd made someone mad or hurt someone's feelings. I'm no longer nineteen; I'm fifty-five. I fully understand sick people do cruel and violent things to other people for no reason; it wasn't my fault."

"How did you eventually get free?"

"He read my poems over and over and over. He'd be quiet for a long time; then he'd read another poem. I never knew when he was going to leave. He said, 'If I made any noise, he'd hurt me.' So, I laid there quietly for hours. Again, I listened for his breathing, and when I thought I heard my door close, I wiggled my hands and feet. I figured if he were still there, he'd tell me to be still. I remember thinking that if he didn't say anything, I might be safe."

"And were you? Were you safe?" she asks.

"You know, I think it was when I didn't report for duty the next morning or when someone finally knocked on my door that I felt safe enough to scream. I screamed with the gag in my mouth. I remember the sound of when they broke down my door. I still couldn't see, and I wasn't 100% positive he wasn't still in the room. I was so afraid when I felt the first touch of someone to cut loose or untie the ties. I'm not sure who it was; it could have been someone from my shop or someone who lived in my barracks. Whoever it was, told me to stay in my bed until the MPs arrived. The ambulance arrived at the same time as the police. I had a little mirror in my room that hung above my dresser; there was lipstick smeared on it. The EMT stood between me and the mirror while he rolled my gurney out of my room. I never saw what it said. Still, to this day, I never received a copy of the report from the MPs. I may not know what it said, but I will always know the smell."

"The smell? Do you mean the smell of him?"

"No. I don't remember what he smelled like; I remember the smell of my lipstick. He used my lipstick to write on my mirror. I'll always remember that smell."

"Did the police take a report at that time?"

"No. Not in my room. The MPs came and took a report when I was in the emergency room. Every part of my body was swabbed, plucked, checked, and tested. Could I please trouble you to hand me another Kleenex?"

"Would you like to take a break, Annamarie?"

"No, I'm fine, thank you. I'd like to get through this and finish."

"Alright. Go ahead," she says.

"Being screwed by the male mentality of the military is what happened next. Two men from the OSI came to see me in the hospital. They said, 'Despite the testimony from the women who broke down the door and untied my arms and legs, they didn't find much evidence to substantiate my claim of rape.' They went on to say, 'Although the pubic hairs collected from my body weren't mine and although there was evidence of penetration, they still can't substantiate rape?' To this day, I can't believe what they said. As recent as today, I get angry at myself for not being more outraged by their comments. If this had happened to me today, I'd respond much differently than how I did back then. I was numb at the time. I was in shock."

At this moment, I feel like a volcano. Words spew out of me like lava; I can't stop. The psychiatrist just listens.

"Yes, I know I was only nineteen years old, but I shouldn't have tolerated their comments. The next thing they did was shatter my faith in humanity. I was furious with my so-called 'military brothers and sisters; my comrades.' While I was still in the hospital receiving treatment for the rape, the MP's and OSI (Operation of Special Intelligence) came into my room to ask even more questions. They didn't have any questions of me as much as they had comments for me. They accused me of making up the story about the attack and the rape in an attempt to be discharged from the Air Force. Seriously, that's what they suggested. I didn't want to get out of the Air Force! I had received approval for cross-training into a new job that wouldn't hurt my back. I told them about the letter from the doctors to authorize my cross-training. Then, the MPs questioned the validity of my back injuries. The doctors treated the vaginal and body pain with pain medication, but I was hurting and pissed at what they were trying to do to me. The Air Force never offered me any counseling. I wasn't provided or given anything. Other than a nurse to take care of my body, no man or woman offered me any help emotionally. Nothing!"

While I was talking, I didn't notice the psychiatrist had picked up her computer and began to type. At this moment, a clicking sound is coming from the keys of her keyboard; it's almost as if she's pounding on the keyboard.

I interrupt her passionate finger pounding to ask, "May I pull out a few documents from the file I brought here today? I have a few things I'd like to show you."

"Certainly, I have copies of everything the VA sent to you in what I call a C-file, but I'd still like to see what you have."

"Here, this is a copy of the report they made while I was in the emergency room. Here are copies of two different DD214s. Here's a copy of the letter from the doctors stating I required cross-training because of back injuries. Here is a copy of the letter requesting the cross-training, and you can see it has was marked as "approved." Here is another copy of that same request that someone has altered. Someone has taken the letter that was approved and has instead circled the word "denied." You can see right here that my commander approved my transfer. Look at this hospital report. In the margin, right near where the doctor and EMTs wrote the word, "rape," someone else has written the word "possible," and tried to change the report. They didn't even try to use the same pen as the doctor who originally wrote the report."

Looking at me with slight confusion, "Where did you get these documents?"

I don't want to lose my momentum, "Wait, wait, I have more. This medical report will show you I received my discharge physical before I was released from the hospital stay for the rape. Somehow I was discharged and out in the civilian world before I had the opportunity to ask questions. I refused to sign a statement that declared I made up the events. The next thing I know, I'm out. I have a completely honorable discharge."

"Can you explain how it was that your medical chart states you had a discharge physical before released from the hospital?"

"That's just it; I can't explain it because I wasn't. You can see the date of my separation is about two weeks after being released from the hospital because of rape."

"How many hours did they take to perform your psych evaluation and conduct your discharge physical?"

"It's been many years now, but I remember going to another office for about fifteen to thirty minutes. That's all."

"You filed for assistance when you discharged in 1977, is that right?"

"Yes. The VA denied my application and said the rape didn't occur."

"Why didn't you appeal?"

"I did. There were no websites in 1977. You talked to people on the phone. I've only recently learned they claimed I had a 'character of behavior disorder,' since birth. When they denied my request for assistance in 1978, I understood it was because they claimed I fabricated the rape. I knew the truth, yet I wasn't emotionally able to fight the VA and the military when I was only nineteen. I had been through a horrible ordeal, and I was a hollowed soldier."

"Did the military document this behavior disorder when you enlisted?"

"No. If I had a disorder, the military wouldn't have accepted me. If a disorder did exist while I was in the service, I wouldn't have received a promotion."

"So, you claim that the disorder appeared when you were assaulted, raped, and discharged?"

"No. I never had a disorder at all. What I had was a rational reaction to being assaulted, raped, and abandoned!"

The doctor suddenly focuses all her attention on her computer. Clicking through files and typing at a crazy speed, she turns back to me and asks, "What was the reason they gave you for the discharge?"

"I was told the discharge was for my protection. I couldn't understand why my commander didn't see to it; I moved to another base. The hospital had just released me, and the reason they gave me for my sudden discharge made no sense to me."

"Do you have any other documents you'd like to share?"

"Yes, I have a lot!"

While organizing all my documents to hand over, we continue our conversation. The doctor asks me to share with her the ways the rape, wrongful discharge, and finally, the treatment I received from the VA has impacted my life.

Her body language changes as soon as I begin to speak. Turning herself to look directly at me, I see the fury she once expressed in her face has reduced, she's calmer. While I share the list of medications I required to manage my depression and anxiety over the years, she only listens while I talk; she doesn't move.

"Immediately upon discharge in October of 1977, my family and childhood doctor put me on my first anti-depressant. In the years that followed, several psychiatrists, psychologists, and counselors worked hard to assist me with the memories of the entire experience. I've been on every medication from Abilify to Wellbutrin; this includes Buspar, Elavil, Lithium, Prozac, Paxil, Flexeril, Tegretol, Seroquil, Effexor XR, and Trileptal. These are just a few of the medications I can recall offhand."

I pause to see if she has a question, comment, or wants me to continue.

"Go on. Please continue," she asks.

"I've masked and covered the memories with massive weight gain and losses. I've experienced periods of denial and low self-esteem. Most of all, I wear a steel armor of humor to attempt to shield myself from any more hurt. Still, the colorless, odorless, and lethal gas of the memories of my attack, rape, and betrayal of the male-dominated Air Force establishment have penetrated the corners of my mind and impacted my life. The injuries I incurred to my back while working in the parachute shop have caused me to require numerous spinal procedures, including cortisone injections, epidural injections, ablation, and major surgery, including a laminectomy."

Pausing again for only a moment, I look over to see if the psychiatrist is still focused on me or if she has gone back to her computer to take more notes. I've depleted over half of the tissues she has in her tissue box; she doesn't seem to mind. I see the time on the clock on the wall, and I'm shocked. I've been talking with her for almost two hours, Aidar must be worried sick. I hope the person scheduled after us doesn't mind.

"If you're up to it, I have a few more questions."

"Up to it? Oh yeah! Yes, I'm up to it. I've been waiting for over three decades for this opportunity. You bet I'm up to it."

"Annamarie, you're an extremely confident woman. Have you always been this way?"

Shaking my head, I can't help but snicker a bit when I say, "No, I can't say it's always been the case. Over the years, I've done a lot of searching in my soul while thinking about my entire military experience. It's the discoveries I've made over the years that moves me to share my story with others. People have held me in high regard, and they often assume I'm always positive and confident. I don't believe anyone is 'always' positive. This awareness is something I'd like for everyone to know. I want to help people understand this, especially when going through a traumatic experience and feeling devastated. No one is positive all the time, and conversely, when you're feeling devastated and negative, we're not going to stay here either. I need to help people with this understanding; that's the only way I can fill the hollowed part of my spirit. I hope to share with people that even the motivator needs motivation."

I pause for a moment to allow her to ask me to stop or carry on. She does exactly this and asks, "Please tell me something you've discovered about yourself?"

"I don't know if it's something I discovered about myself, as much as it's something I discovered about how I was thinking about the man who raped me and the entire situation altogether. One day I stopped and thought about what the rapist took from me. For years I believed the first thing the rapist had stolen from me was my self-confidence. I thought the rapist took even more away from me than just my self-confidence. I lost my trust in others, trust in life, trust in systems, and anything you once believed were stable and solid. I mean, think about this for a moment. When police officers arrive at a crime scene and discover a dead body, they examine the body to see how the victim was injured and killed. When they examine this body and see the impression and indention of a watch or a ring, but the watch and ring are missing, they know those two items were stolen. Following my rape, when I was alone and opened my eyes for the first time, I made this same assessment into my spirit. I immediately discovered my confidence was missing. Various edges of my core were wounded; but, it was most noticeable that only an indention remained where my confidence once stood. I searched everywhere for it, but I couldn't find it. I tried to find it in other people. I thought if someone had enough confidence in me, then I'd feel confident too. I was hopeful that I could claim the confidence they had in me as my own, but it wasn't there. I searched for it in superficial activities and light conversation over a glass of wine, but it wasn't there either. I couldn't find it in shopping centers, jewelry stores, or fancy resorts. The more I searched to find it in my physical appearance, or the affections of other men, the more apparent it became that I had lost it for good. I mastered the smile. I discovered, the more I smiled, the more comfortable others were in watching me live my life. My outward smile made other people happy, but it wasn't sincere; I believed someone else had it. It was important for other people to see me pushing through the terrible experience. My family and friends needed to see me smile, and I needed to see them happy. I tried the practice of 'Fake it until you make it,' but it was only good on my exterior. It helped create good habits, but it didn't help me for the long haul. It was the 'fake it' part of the practice that wasn't reliable; it just didn't fit me. I tried to master the art of applying a fake mask of 'acceptance.' I put on the front as if it was sheer make-up from Cover-girl. All the while, deep down in my core, I believed my true confidence was lost forever. I was the queen of living vicariously through the achievements of others. I'm now sure this is why I became an inspirational speaker. It was glorious to lead others down the path to great success. I flourished while giving others the tools they needed to be positive and confident.

"Then one day, I stumbled upon a piece of my confidence, and I thought, 'There you are! That's where I put you.' It hit home when I repeated the words, 'That's where I put you!' Have you ever put something in a safe place and told yourself you'd remember where you put it and then only forget?"

Laughing, she says, "Yes. I know what you're talking about; I just did this the other day."

41

"Well, It's similar to when we know a storm is approaching, we take our valuables and put them somewhere safe. When we leave our home on vacation, we hide our valuables safely out of sight. If I'm even the tiniest bit stressed, I'll completely forget where I put my valuables. When I can't find them, I consider them gone forever.

"Today, at the age of 57, I have a different opinion regarding what a tragedy can take from me. Specifically, in my case, I know the man who raped me AND the military justice system that didn't give me protection shattered my confidence. I've had to find it in myself and put it back together. I believe in the moment of my rape; I reacted quickly to protect who I am; preserve my spirit. My confidence was utterly shattered, not stolen. I believe in the rape and crisis; I quickly tucked my confidence into a safe place in my soul. It was never lost; I had only forgotten where I had placed the precious pieces. Once I realized I still had all the pieces inside of myself, I had to dig deep and work hard to put it back together. I became a master confidence hunter. I had to give little pieces of my trust to people to develop the confidence to trust myself again. I've learned to search within myself to pull all the shattered pieces together.

"When I'm helping other people to be confident and successful, I become confident. While I tell other people that I have confidence in them, I can pull the once fragmented pieces of confidence into the completely whole woman I am right now. Sure, now and then, I'll still stumble on chips of broken confidence; but now it's easier to recognize my fears and put the confidence right back where it belongs.

"I stopped to ask myself why it was; the confidence and faith others had in me didn't make me feel like I could succeed. I couldn't become confident until I gave it away. I had first to give someone a little of my trust before I learned to trust myself. I know this may sound crazy, but it isn't until we pass along and share a gift that we're able to receive fully. It's a long answer, but

I felt it needed explaining. I believe that my rapist stole nothing. I am whole.

"Let me make one more point, and I'll stop talking."

The doctor says, "No, no, no. Your perception is interesting; please go on."

"Well, one day, I thought about my belief that the man who raped me ruined my life. I started thinking about what my role or responsibility was in making my life great. I can't go back in time and change what happened. I can't change the fact my faith, confidence, and trust was crushed, but I can change my life from this day forward. Every time I thought about the rape and what followed, I let those thoughts ruin my outlook. The rape and wrongful discharge happened years before. I was the one who was ruining my day and letting it impact my life. I recognized that every day I continued to allow it to be a bad day; I let him take another day away from me. When I'd wake up in the morning and start my day by thinking of my experience in the military and what the VA did to me, I'd be picking them and my rapist, up in my arms and carrying him with me. It felt like I was walking over to him and giving him my happiness; he wasn't coming to me. I decided I wasn't going to let him win; I wasn't going to let the military take away any more of my life's dreams than they already had.

"Now, I still have a lot of trouble with certain scenarios frightening me and making me react differently than what I'd like, but being afraid of a ghost isn't one of them. I hope to understand why I'm jumpier than most people. Our son likes to startle me because I jump easily, but I won't allow the past to diminish any of my confidence and power."

"You are an insightful woman Annamarie. I wish you all the best. I can see why you're an inspirational speaker. Maybe I'll be able to hear you speak one day; I'd like that very much. If you don't mind, may I have copies of all the documents you brought with you today?"

"Of course, but I thought you said the VA sent you a C-file with copies of everything I have?"

"Well, there may be one or two pages I can't locate. If you don't object, I'd like to have copies of what you've brought with you."

Finally! When my psychological exam finishes, Aidar comes into the room; his cheeks are tense, rosy, and filled with blood.

Looking at me with deep concern, he asks,

"Honey, are you okay?"

"Yes. I'm fine. Like we discussed, I was myself. I told the truth; that's all I can do."

Aidar spends another thirty minutes with the psychiatrist. I reminded myself that I'm not the only person impacted by rape and discharge. For the past thirty-three years, Aidar has suffered the effects of my rape as they've rippled through me. Even Austin has paid the price for the experience. I'm exhausted; I feel as if the doctor pressed the instant rewind and replay button in my brain. While I sit here and wait for Aidar to finish with his interview, painful memories rapidly fire off with my thoughts. My neck is clammy; my clothes stick like paste on my body.

The conversation between Aidar and me on the drive home is a repeat of everything I discussed with the psychiatrist. He concludes our conversation by asking, "So, what do you think? How do you think it went?"

"I have absolutely no idea. Based on how she took notes, I think it went well. I also think the fact I supplied her with more documents than the VA did. I think she was surprised. The VA told her everything she needed, and all of the documents they had were in the C-file; but they weren't. I had a bunch of information, documentation, and proof they didn't give her. I don't think that made her happy. She said she'd submit her findings, and I'll be notified by mail. So, we just wait."

CHAPTER 3

★ ★ ★ ★ ★

Vindication – 2014

I'm proud of the woman I've become and I value my name or my character. I'm not going to let anyone slander my good name, especially when they aren't telling the truth.

Θ   Θ   Θ

My parents always told me that "patience is a virtue," if this is true, I'm not very virtuous. Walking up and down our driveway to pick up mail has become routine. Each day begins with feelings of hope the VA's decision will arrive, and concludes with feelings void of satisfaction. I confess not every moment is negative. Despite the intense moments of high anxiety or the increase in the number of visits to a therapist, I've noticed how beautiful our property's nature resembles a well-conducted symphony. The variety of oak trees lining our driveway makes it easy to witness the changing of the seasons. Each tree is as separate as a single instrument in an orchestra. The precise timing and release of acorns is a masterpiece; the maestro is God. I can imagine that each strong gust of wind is God sweeping a huge baton to direct the beautiful music of nature. One swish is a cue to the trees on my right to drop their nuggets and decorate the earth near my feet. The next sweep of his baton signals the trees on my left to hold their acorns until a warmer day tightly. My walk's speed and tempo may change daily, but the joy I receive from each unique song remains the same. Marching through this process of the appeal hasn't made me tired of nature; I will always enjoy the walk. Although I'm often impatient, I remember the military motto to "hurry up and wait."

The VA sends so many letters and documents; I decided to share some of my story with Ramon, our mailman. He's now invested and anxious for a decision. This morning Ramon says, "Here's another lightweight envelope for you, Annamarie. It looks as if it's from the VA. Hopefully, it's the notice you've been waiting for."

"Hey, Ramon! If you continue to deliver the 'lightweight' envelopes, I'll have enough paper to plaster an entire wall in my office. It isn't that I don't want to walk down the driveway to visit with you, but I'm waiting for a 'heavy' envelope. Can you please make that happen?"

Ramon replies with a quick smile and wink. "I'll see what I can do. In the meantime, here you go."

Ramon is right; it's another thin request. This time they want me to see another one of their doctors; it's an orthopedist. I thought my examinations were finished, but now they'd like an assessment of my back. I'm happy to oblige. This doctor is welcome to examine my spine, measure the scars from my previous surgery, and order all the x-rays and MRIs they desire. In case my scars don't provide ample evidence to validate my claim of injury, I'm happy to provide thirty-five years of treatment records to document the surgery, invasive procedures, and therapies. These treatments have been necessary for an attempt to relieve the pain and repair the damage I incurred while working in the parachute shop.

The last eighteen months feel as though the hands of time are stuck in 1977. I have no concern with the review of my back injuries; it's the report from the investigative psychiatrist that has me curious. The orthopedist can look at the exams and evidence to see my back injuries; he can go as far back as 1977 and read the reports to recommend I be removed from the parachute shop and re-trained. Considering my experience, no one can blame me for feeling skeptical about the psychiatric review; her review is less black and white. I wonder if this new investigation will finally uncover the truth of my claim. I'm cynical, cautiously optimistic, yet I remain reluctant to trust a military bureaucracy that abandoned me and left me emotionally bleeding in the trenches.

Aidar tries his best to comfort me. I need so much reassurance the psychiatric investigator wasn't part of the military or Veterans Administration. I've submitted all the forms required by the VA, and I've signed a release to confirm I have no more evidence to provide. It's completely out of my hands; again, I have no control. We've fought the fight, and now we wait. The appointment at the independent orthopedist is uneventful and dull. I bend over and touch my toes upon request. I flex and fold my body in the precise spots where they tell me, and I submit the records for thirty years of back surgery and treatments.

Every morning I enjoy a cup of coffee; maybe two. I prefer to have it easy up, black with no cream, no sugar. For the past seven days, the coffee tastes bitter. I use the same brand of coffee beans, the same process, and the same coffee machine. Yet, the coffee tastes bitter. I've just spent twenty minutes looking for my glasses, and I found them on top of my head. Something is out of balance. I can't shake this feeling as though something is awry. I'm not psychic, though I wish I were. Something just doesn't feel right.

It's two o'clock in the afternoon, time to make my walk down the driveway to see what Ramon may have left in the mailbox.

The mailbox has a security lock, and the small key that secures it requires more pushing than usual. The lock feels stuck. My thumb struggles to turn the key. It feels as if a letter or envelope has jammed the locking clip. Finally! The key turns, and the heavyweight of all the mail pushes the door open. Smashed inside with all the envelopes from the credit card companies soliciting applications for credit, marketing materials from local businesses and political ads from candidates seeking re-election is a thick white envelope. Stamped in blue ink on the upper left corner of this heavy package is a familiar return address. At last, the decision by the Veterans Administration on my appeal has finally arrived.

I've thought about this moment a hundred times. I've seen myself reading every imaginable verdict. Fumbling with all the different-sized envelopes, the excitement from receiving this heavy one from the VA causes me to drop ALL the mail. Everything falls to the black asphalt of the driveway. The only envelope I bother to pick up is the letter from the VA; the rest of the mail can sit on the ground. No matter how hard I try to tear through the thick paper of the envelope, I can't get through. I squat next to a sticky rosemary bush and try again to get through the envelope by using my teeth. Nope, my teeth can't get through the paper either. The small pieces of gravel on the driveway are grinding into my legs, but I pay it no attention. Then I make a MacGyver connection. I'm determined to open this envelope and read it by myself. I take the little mailbox key and poke it through the small cellophane window on the front of the envelope, revealing my name and address. Finally!

To: Annamarie Ibrahim

Blah, blah, blah, blah, blah, blah, blah.

I don't want to read the paragraphs about the "great care" devoted to reviewing my file; I only want the decision. My eyes scan the paragraphs and skip past the majority of words. I only focus on the words written in bold type.

What We Decided

We determined that the following conditions were related to your military service, so service connection has been granted:

1. Service connection for low back strain with degenerative disc disease is granted, effective date is February 7, 2013.
2. Service Connection for Post-Traumatic Stress Disorder (PTSD) for Military Sexual Trauma (MST) is granted, effective date is February 7, 2013.
3. Rating decision approved August 22, 1978 did not contain a clear and unmistakable error.

Bitter-sweet! I feel as if I have a big piece of bitter-sweet chocolate in my mouth. I'd like to let it melt slowly. I'd like to soak in every word but my eyes dart back and forth on the page like lasers ripping through the paper in search of the final decision. They agree the back injury occurred while I was serving in the Air Force. They agree I've suffered from Post-Traumatic Stress Disorder (PTSD) for the Military Sexual Trauma (MST). They're going to give me benefits that date back to the day I filed this claim in 2013.

"This is wrong! I filed my claim in January, 1978. I filed a claim for help a few weeks after my discharge. Yet…wait, wait, wait. They don't agree they made a mistake in 1978 when they denied me any assistance. How can they agree I was injured and raped while in the military but they didn't make a mistake in 1978? It was the VA who stood firm in the position and informed me in 1978 that I was never raped and I was

abruptly discharged because it was determined that I had a "character of behavior disorder" since birth. Really?"

I'm on fire! My thighs don't feel their usual burn as I walk back up the driveway to the house. I'm angry, upset, happy, and confused. Over the years, I've convinced myself it didn't matter what others believed or didn't believe about my rape. I knew the truth, and that's what mattered. I told myself their acceptance and approval of me didn't matter, but I can see now that it did. I want to shout out loud, but I'm afraid the neighbors might be concerned if I begin yelling. I want to shout out loud to the VA and say, *"In your face. Take that in your face. I told you the truth in 1977 when they discharged me; I told you I was raped."* I'm angry they didn't believe me when I was in the hospital and needing help. I'm satisfied they can no longer deny the evidence.

Looking at the compensation, I'm tempted to shout, *"It's too little too late."* The money I'll receive from the disability award won't reimburse me for the years of depression, frustration, and anxiety. My emotions are mixed up. I feel joy, anger, and confusion. I'm joyful, yet I'm sobbing. I don't feel disappointed or satisfied. Feeling like this isn't what I expected. The months of sleepless nights thinking about my reaction to the decision have been for nothing. I predicted I'd feel happy when they admitted I was raped and wrongfully discharged. I thought I'd be disappointed if they determined their decision in 1978 still stands. I never considered my emotional reaction to both a positive and negative result. I'm feeling all mixed up. I'm both ecstatic and angry.

Whack! The heavy stack of documents I received from the VA makes a loud noise when I slam them against the kitchen counter. Austin and Aidar stop what they're doing to turn around to see what's going on.

Austin is the first one to ask, "Mom, what happened to your face?"

"Nothing. Why?"

"Your mascara is all over the place." Laughing, he continues to say, "You have black streaks running everywhere. Go look in a mirror."

"Well, I guess it's because the mail came in today."

Austin asks, "What do you mean; the mail came in? Doesn't it come in almost every day?"

"Yes, but it came in today, and we finally have a decision."

Spinning around on his heels, Aidar closes the refrigerator door and asks, "Well! Are you happy?"

I find it telling how Aidar asks about my happiness before asking about the decision. He's more concerned about how I feel and not the decision. To him, the decision doesn't compare to my satisfaction and happiness. No matter what the decision could be, he just wants me to be happy.

My only response is, "I don't know. Maybe yes. But not really. I know this doesn't make any sense. I don't feel anything like what I thought I'd feel."

As the three of us walk over to the couch to sit down, Aidar stops to give me a long, firm hug. Sitting side by side, together, we read the decision one word at a time. He frequently reaches over to rub my shoulder or pat my thigh. Giving me a sweet kiss on my cheek he whispers, "You did it, honey. You won."

"I didn't win. We won. We did this together. All of us."

Aidar opens a chilled bottle of my favorite champagne to celebrate. He raises his glass to make a toast and says,

"You're beautiful inside and out. You're wonderful, and you're far more than just a survivor. You're a conqueror. Your perseverance and commitment to see this through is precisely the example we've always wanted to show Austin. That's exactly what you've done. You're a success in all that you do. You never gave up, and you've endured the BS and always held on to the truth. I'm so proud of you."

Austin follows the comment with, "Me too, Mom!"

The champagne doesn't taste good. Maybe I just need some time to digest the decision; it isn't sitting right in my bones. I started this fight with the original objective to help others find the strength to use their voice. I was hoping to be an example of perseverance and resiliency. I was hoping other victims would see I've been a success in life despite my experience. I never let anything hold me back. Because I opened this appeal, I have demonstrated it's never too late to confront fear and win. However, I'm not finished! I'm going to get back in the ring and finish this fight. I won the round but not the match. I'm going to talk with the one man who inspired me to file this appeal tomorrow morning. I'm going to see Tom, the VSO from the Solano County Department Veterans Services.

A few days have passed since I received the decision from the VA. When I finally have a chance to meet with Tom, he reaches out to shake my hand. I don't want a handshake, I want a hug; I want a BIG hug.

"You did it, Annamarie. You won. The VA 'finally' acknowledged the rape, and I'm so thrilled. Your persistence will help so many other men and women with their claims because they can refer to your win and site it as an example. I know it wasn't easy for you. You've helped me too."

"I wouldn't be where I am today without you, Tom. You challenged me and supported me all the way. You also restored my faith in a lot of areas. I've learned not to pre-judge a system any more than I've ever judged a person. I'm forever grateful."

"You know Annamarie; now you'll receive disability benefits. It's not going to be a lot, but what's important for you is that you'll also have medical benefits. Benefits are a big deal. I'm so happy for you, and I'm especially proud of you. Over the last two years, I witness what this appeal put you through; you're one tough lady."

The VA acknowledges my PTSD, and the injury to my back is accurately documented. Tom encourages me to appeal and challenge the VA's decision about the original date of the claim. I initially filed a claim only a few short weeks after I was discharged in 1978, not in 2013. He prepares me for a long wait on this appeal; the backlog of claims is long. The wait will be a minimum of two to four years.

As I'm about to walk out of the door of Tom's office, he says a similar statement to the one he made when we first met. "Annamarie, I'd like to change something I said to you a couple of years ago."

"Alright. Go ahead," I say.

"I once told you I wasn't positive of what may have happened to you, but YOUR voice may help those who aren't able to speak up for themselves. Now I'm going to tell you, I'm absolutely positive of what happened to you and now, so is the VA. They can't deny it. I'm also positive YOUR voice will help those who aren't able to speak up for themselves. Annamarie, I know you're tough enough to see this through. Will you hang tough with me a little longer?"

We're both smiling from ear to ear, and without hesitation, I say, "I will. The VA made a clear and unmistakable error in their denial of my request for benefits in 1978. We're going to prove it. I'm still angry; they claim I had a 'character of behavior disorder' since birth. It's just wrong. I may not have had the strength, courage, or support when I was nineteen, but I'm no longer a scared little girl, and I'm not alone in my fight."

"Annamarie, you're far from alone; we're here to support you. Would you like to read the report filed by the psychiatrist who examined you?"

While I step back into his office, I'm reaching out my hand and wiggling my fingers to say, "Please give it to me."

I've been chomping at the bit to know her opinion and read her findings. I'm excited, anxious, and elated Tom has printed a copy for me to take home. I chew on every word and digest her opinion slowly. My eyes rest on the frequent phrases where she shines a light on the fact the VA didn't supply ALL the documentation as they claimed they had within their C-file. I'm so gratified to read, "The Veteran is an honest and reliable historian. She fought to gain access to her 'lost' military records for over eight months. Once she got her congressman involved, she received her records within 24 hours. The Veteran's emotional presentation was consistent with a victim of sexual assault. In addition, the details offered by the Veteran are believable and substantiated in the medical records she brought, but that were not included in the C-file."

I read more and more comments to validate my claim and dispute the VA's initial claim in 1978, claiming there was no evidence or documentation to substantiate a rape. The VA's claim that I had a mental defect since birth is incorrect, unfounded, and irresponsible.

Grabbing on to the wooden arm of the chair in front of Tom's desk, I slide my body down to sit and continue reading.

"According to the medical records obtained by the Veteran, she was in the hospital for three or four days. The Veteran's medical records also indicated bruising resulting from being tied to the bed. These records were also absent from the C-File. It is the opinion of this investigator that the Veteran was sexually assaulted and that this assault and the subsequent treatment she received by the US Air Force traumatized her deeply."

I feel like she heard me; the psychiatrist heard me. The 'independent' investigative psychiatrist 'they' selected has read and listened to my truth. I hear my inner voice, shouting, "*Go! Get em. Go fight for me Annamarie.*"

I read on with even more excitement and fury.

"She brought with her the medical records, which were more inclusive than those provided for review in the C-file. For example, there's an emergency visit dated September 9, 1977 where she was attacked in the park and an attempted rape occurred. There's also a medical record dated October 5, 1977 but not one mention of the rape was included. Nor was there a mention of her three to four day hospital stay. She had these records with her and the examiner reviewed them."

I slap my right hand down on the top of Tom's desk. The sound of my palm hitting the glass top covering the wood is drowned out by my voice as I shout, "Yes! Yes! Yes!"

Pausing for a moment to look up at Tom, I see him standing tall with his arms folded across his chest; his smile spans his face's entire width.

All three pages of this report are filled with comments to support my claim. All of the pages are full of admonishments of the VA for not providing all the documentation in the C-file. One of the most significant comments in the psychiatrist report is her statement to dispute the VA's claim. She disputes their analysis that I had an immature personality disorder since birth that required my discharge. The investigator could see the documentation that the only time a disorder was noted was *after* my rape.

Sixteen months ago, old emotional wounds were ripped open when I stormed out of the community center. I thought the experience of my rape was closed over with scabs and callouses; I was wrong. While immersing myself in my career as a motivational speaker, I masked so many feelings and emotions surrounding this assault, rape, and betrayal. By facing the demons within me, I've been able to process my entire military experience better. While addressing these demons, I was able to identify the weaker spots in my life that had become infected from the lack of proper therapy. Re-opening this allows me to seek appropriate treatment focused on PTSD and MST. I'm now able to recognize the depth and severity of my pain and treat it appropriately.

When I've shared my experience with other male friends of mine, many of them feel a need to apologize on behalf of other men for my rape. I appreciate their comments. However, I don't believe an apology from anyone other than the rapist is necessary. I know there are a lot of hurtful and despicable women; I'm not one of them. When another woman does something horrible to another person, I don't apologize for all women. Not all women hurt, but neither do all men. I believe there are good people and bad people; it isn't necessary to be gender-specific. I won't close my eyes, and blindly trust all people, trust all policies, trust all agencies and systems. I try my best to weigh all circumstances against what I know to be good, bad, fair, and kind.

CHAPTER 4

★ ★ ★ ★ ★

Triggers

When a fire is left unattended, it can burn down an entire forest and destroy many lives. Yet, when I respect the flame's power, I can use it to warm me, cook my food, and give me light in the dark. A little respect and understanding can go a long way.

Θ   Θ   Θ

The crepe myrtle tree at the corner of our street is bursting with blossoms. Like popcorn, the white flowers are bulging out of their buds to pop out. This bright white color does not blend into the blue sky; these flowers stand out to catch my attention. It's early April, and there is no doubt it is truly a spring day. I've ironed my white pants to hold a crisp seam, which stands out in total opposition to the well-worn but very comfortable flip-flops on my feet. If I take a moment to think about it, this opposition is like my attitude right now. I don't want to make this drive I'm about to make. My outfit isn't as crucial to my psychological state as the yellow manila envelope

I'm carrying in my hand. I call the contents of the envelope my "marching orders." Documents to authorize my medical benefits must be hand-carried to the closest VA military facility, and for me, this is Travis Air Force Base. In my memory, I hear the sound of boots pounding the pavement. I hear the Drill Sargent's bellowing cries, *"Left, Right, Left, Right."* My first payment of benefits has arrived with a notice to report to my home's closest VA military facility. It's time to pick up my Veteran ID card and a VA military ID card to enter the base. Travis Air Force Base in Fairfield is nearby, and it's here that veterans from all branches of the military receive their care. The time has come for me to meet with my newly assigned primary medical doctor.

The drive from our home to the base doesn't require the GPS in our car. Huge green signs with reflective paint stand on the highway's sides, pointing all drivers to Travis Air Force Base. The closer I get to the base, the more aware I become of the bumper stickers that proudly adorn most of the cars and trucks around me. "Semper-Fi, Vietnam War Survivor and USAF" are just a few of the brightly colored stickers sealing in the pride of the driver. Blinking my eyes to focus on what I see in the distance, it's a backup of cars. The closer I get to the guard gate and the base's entrance, the straight road suddenly curves and twists from right to left. If the curves don't slow people down, the extra-high speed bumps will. My car is shaking with each tire's rise and fall as they independently roll over the bumps.

I'm filled with panic when, without warning, my stomach cramps, and breakfast makes its way back through my throat. I pull my car to the right and stop. I can sit in a sauna or lay in the sun without ever breaking a sweat, but now my hair is saturated. My scalp tingles as sweat rolls through the strands of my hair and gathers at my temples and hairline. If I sit here in my car for a few minutes, I hope this feeling will pass. Once again, I pull into traffic, but I'm over-ruled by my body and throw-up. I've enough digestive issues to know this feeling isn't coming from my stomach; it's coming from my heart. All I think *is "This is craziness, this reaction isn't logical! Annamarie, you're not afraid of a doctor. You go to doctor appointments all the time. You stand up before thousands of people; one doctor is a piece of cake. Now put the car into drive and get on this stupid base!"*

Despite my internal desire to run, I push myself to drive onto the base where I manage to find my way to the waiting room of my doctor. Tattered and expired magazines line the top of the glass tables. The types of magazines make it evident that not many women visit this waiting area. I can only find magazines on men's fitness, cars, and careers in the military. I can't find a single copy of something I'd be interested in reading, yet I pick one up and mindlessly fumble through the sticky pages.

Sitting to my left is a gentleman who looks to be around my age. When I look up from reading my magazine, he catches my eye and says, "What branch of the service were you in?"

"I was in the Air Force."

As if doubting my response, he asks, "Really? How many tours did you do?"

"Oh shit! Oh shit! What's he talking about? Tours? Tours? I don't understand the word tours."

I know the puzzled look on my face must confuse him, but I legitimately don't know how to answer it. I'm not connecting the word "tours" with what I experienced while serving in the Air Force. Decades have passed since I was in a military environment; military lingo isn't commonplace for me. I don't readily associate the word "tours" with the number of enlisted periods I served. I remember what it means now, but at the moment, he asked me, he may have well asked me, "What color was your first blanket in kindergarten for nap time?" The truthful answer to his question is that the military prevented me from completing one single tour. I'm concerned that if I tell him I served less than one tour, he might ask me, "why?" I'm not sure how to answer this question, either. I don't know if I want to answer this question in this military setting. Several other middle-aged men come into the waiting room.

When I look around the entire area, I notice I'm the only woman. Just as I'm about to answer this man's question, a young Airman wearing military fatigues comes and sits next to me on my right. This young man has a pleasant smile and looks to be no more than 20 years old; he's accompanying an older gentleman.

Long strands of silver tinsel hanging from the air conditioner vent start to move. Despite the moving glitz, my chest is constricting from lack of oxygen. I can't breathe. My heart is once again pounding out of control, and my throat is tightening like Chinese handcuffs holding two fingers together. I can barely swallow.

Thirty-eight years have passed since my rape, yet the moment this young Airman sits down next to me, I travel back in time at the speed of light. I'm yanked back into an emotion I believe is unrealistic and unacceptable. No matter what my logical mind things about this emotion, it's none the less undeniable. Faintly, off in the distance, I hear someone calling my name. A brief moment has passed; I never answered the question about the number of tours I served in the Air Force. In that short period, I mentally regressed from a fifty-year-old woman to a petrified and panicked nineteen-year-old girl. Coming to my rescue by calling out my name is a nurse; it's time for me to move back to the exam room. I've escaped the conversation and simultaneously avoided this young man in uniform who triggered me in ways I don't understand.

Contributing to the stress is the bad news from the scale she uses to weigh me. *Dang!* The numbers from the scale add more stress to raise the already high numbers on the blood pressure cuff. The wrinkled and torn tissue paper laid across the exam table compounds all of these subliminal stressors. A new piece of paper hasn't been rolled out for me; this piece is leftover from the previous patient. I'm not a neat freak, but this disturbs me. I don't want to make a fuss, but I want it changed. The nurse doesn't attempt to change the paper and roll out a new sheet, so I'll do it myself. I don't want to sit on paper where someone else may have sat their naked butt. I'm not going to ask her if she'd "mind" if I changed the tissue paper. I'm just going to do it. No harm, no foul. I change the paper, and she calmly says, "The doctor will be in shortly to see you."

Three knocks on the door warn me the doctor is about to enter. The door swings open, and the doctor asks, "Do you mind if I take a moment to review your medical history?"

"No, by all means, take all the time you need."

I can't help but wonder why he didn't review my file before he walked into the room. Now I just sit here in silence while watching him read. The doctor doesn't read quietly, he hems and haws while reading my medical history. Taking off his glasses, he starts to chew on the tip of their arm that goes around the back of his ear to hold them on his head. He tips his side from one side to the other while making strange sounds like "ah-ha" and "hum" that I speak up and ask,

"Is there something troubling you? Perhaps I can explain."

"No, everything looks good. So tell me, Mrs. Ibrahim, how are you doing today?"

"In general, I'm well, but at this moment thing's kind of suck. I have no idea what's happening to me. I'm a very controlled and intelligent woman, but I'm not feeling right. It's difficult to breathe."

In the file sitting in front of him are all the pieces to a complicated physical and emotional puzzle known as "*ME.*" My doctors and specialists in the civilian world don't have access to the entire puzzle. My previous doctors were only given one puzzle piece at a time, and it didn't contain any information about my rape. It's challenging to assemble an entire puzzle when you have no idea what the finished puzzle would look like when completed. Even if one of my previous doctors knew about my time in the Air Force, they certainly didn't know about all the details. Right here and right now, the doctor can witness the total effects of my PTSD. Just by driving onto a military base and sitting in the waiting room of this doctor, my mind has sucked me back into a dark place and contained no light. Logic has no place in this dark space. I know the man who raped me would be my age at least, but rational thinking is absent from me right now. For some odd reason, I think the twenty-year-old man who just sat next to me in the lobby could be my rapist. Like the man who raped me, this man's uniform made the same swishing sound when he moved. The squeaking sound his boots made as he moved across the linoleum tiles was identical to the sound I remember in 1977 on the floor of my barracks. I've always referred to my depression as a dark place that feels heavy. What I need now is some air. I need air and bright natural light.

The doctor reaches out to gently squeeze my upper arm. It appears to me he wants to convey an emotion of trust and understanding. Before speaking, he sits down on the little round stool with tiny wheels. "Let's just visit for a while," he says.

In the middle of telling the doctor about the experience I had while trying to drive onto the base, and what I just felt when the young Airman sat next to me, the doctor interrupts me and says, "Mrs. Ibrahim, what you experienced is a trigger to your PTSD. Your logical brain knows the man who raped you isn't still twenty years old today. Your memory and sub-conscious mind aren't always logical." He continues and asks, "Have you had experiences like this in the past?"

Shaking my head up and down, I say, "Yes, but not like this."

"Alright. Let's take some big breaths together. I'd like to try an exercise with you. Are you up for that?"

I eagerly reply, "Absolutely!"

"Would you prefer I call you Mrs. Ibrahim, or may I call you Annamarie?"

"Yes, please. I much prefer Annamarie," I say with a smile.

"Let's take a few more deep breaths. Breathe in through your nose and out your mouth. Focus on the breath as it comes in and moves through your body and out your nose. Okay, let's take a few more in, and I'd like you to breathe in for the count of four. Now hold your breath for the count of four and slowly let your breath out for four counts."

Trying to bring a little fun into the conversation, I say, "I feel like you're going to try to hypnotize me."

"I assure you," he says. "That won't happen. Can you please tell me the color of these walls?"

"They're green."

Wanting me to be more specific, he asks, "What shade of green?"

"They're light green."

"What's the color of my shirt under my lab coat?"

"It's blue. It's dark blue," I say.

"What else do you see on my shirt?"

"Buttons, I see some white buttons," I say.

"How many buttons do you see?"

I snapped back, "I can only see two buttons, but there are probably more as it continues underneath your coat."

"No, only tell me what you see. Don't let your imagination go beyond what you see and what you know."

Sounding a bit more contrite, I add, "Okay! Then I only see two buttons."

In the corner of the office is a small sink with soap and a stack of white paper towels.

"Annamarie, please walk over to the sink and turn on the cold water. Put your hands in the water and tell me what you feel."

"What do you mean by what I feel? What I feel on my hands or what I'm feeling in my thoughts or emotions when I put my hands under the water?"

"I want you to stay focused only on what you feel on your hands. Stay present on what you're doing right now. Please put your hands in the water. Focus on the feeling of the water and share your thoughts with me."

Sliding my hands under the stream of water, I focus only on the feeling and say, "It's cold, and it feels nice."

"What else do you feel?"

Feeling a bit more expressive, I reply, "The water is bubbly, it moves when I move my hands underneath the flow. It feels a little bit like the tiny bubbles in champagne."

"Can you control the direction of the water flow?" he asks.

Smiling, I nod my head up and down. "I see what you're doing."

"I'm not doing anything other than directing your conscious mind to be more present. When you're experiencing a flash-back or when you have a trigger to your PTSD, you become lost in a memory. It can be helpful to focus on exactly what you see and touch. The more specific and detailed you can be in your descriptions, the more you'll stay in the moment and reduce your anxiety. This is only one example of the many techniques and tools available to you for PTSD and MST."

"This helps. Please teach me some more," I beg.

"I'm not specialized in this area of treatment or therapy. There are far better doctors than me to help you. Here's a brochure on the programs. I'm happy to write you a referral."

Grabbing on to the brochure, I read it thoroughly. It almost as if I'm looking to find a solution to get my rapist out of my head. With each description of common symptoms of PTSD and MST, I see a connection to a diagnosis. Within some of the stories I read in this brochure, I immediately discover more compassion for myself. It's "refreshing" to realize that many of the reactions I've had in my life are perfectly "normal." My responses to numerous triggers never need to be judged; I only need to observe myself. I want to learn more.

For thirty-eight years, I've told a rehearsed story, a very well-rehearsed story. I've told the story about my rape in a memorized fashion, almost like a song. Children recite the alphabet by associating it with a melody. When I ask a child, "What comes after the letter J?" they often go back to the letter H and sing it again. I've never hesitated to tell my story, but I do it with little emotion or understanding. It's similar to only making love with the lights off. In the dark, you can't see everything very clearly. I've been able to hide from myself emotionally. I haven't shared my story with many people in the full light.

The doctor continues to give me a routine physical, schedule all the standard blood work, and send me on my way. It's sure a lot easier to drive off this base than it was getting on.

Immediately, I sign up for the counseling services offered by the VA to specifically address the unique impacts of MST. When I begin to allow more light to come into my life, I can see the issues and triggers. The light allows me to see where I'd like to grow and change. The analogy of needing light reminds me of one of the stories I share with my audience when I'm speaking about stress management and overcoming fears. For all my childhood years, my mom was a seamstress. Ladies would come to our home, where she designed and made custom dresses. My bedroom also served as the room where she did her sewing.

Back then, ladies didn't wear slacks too often, and my mom had a dress mannequin. She fit the dresses onto this mannequin to make sure it fit before the ladies would come over to try it on. The mannequin had no head, no arms, and no legs. It just stood there on one single pole with four pegs extending out for balance. I thought the pegs were the toes. When it came time to go to bed to sleep, my parents put the mannequin in my closet and shut the door. This mannequin tortured me when it was in the dark closet. My parents told me that one evening, shortly after they put me to bed, I ran out of my room and jumped into my dad's arms. At the top of my lungs, I screamed, "Let her out! Let her out so I can see her!" The mannequin didn't move if I could see her. When I could see her, she didn't chase me. Even if my room only had a dim light, she didn't torture me like she did when she was in the dark closet and left to my imagination. I discovered that when we keep our fears in the dark and don't bring them up into the light, they torment and torture us.

Counseling sessions and workshops help me to open more doors to the traumas of my life. If only I had the proper counseling thirty years ago, twenty years ago or even last year. Like carving into a piece of wood, you need to use the right tool for the job. I know you don't use a screwdriver when you need to hammer a nail. A screwdriver might be able to get the job done, but it's going to take a lot longer, you'll likely get hurt in the process. I've had years of therapy and counseling, but it wasn't for the right issue. I didn't have the right tools to cope and move forward in a healthy way.

A friend in our neighborhood works for the American Red Cross. They have an annual meeting to recognize local heroes in Solano County, and she asked me to speak. As I stand up here at the podium, I see one of my heroes sitting in the audience. It's our congressman who assisted me in obtaining my medical records from the Veterans Administration. We've never met in person, but he's quite familiar with my name. My speech is humorous, inspirational, and educational. During my speech, I don't say anything about my experience in the Air Force.

When I finish my speech, people line up to say thank you and shake my hand. I see our congressman standing in line; he's slowly making his way up to the front. The moment he says my name, it's clear that he has a different purpose for waiting in line.

"Annamarie Ibrahim. Are you the same Annamarie Ibrahim, my staff, assisted in obtaining some records and filing a claim with the VA?"

I can't help but smile and confess, "Yes, it's me."

He reaches out to shake my hand, and he squeezes tightly. "I didn't know you were a speaker," he says. "You're great. You're excellent."

I feel slightly embarrassed, yet honored. "Thank you very much. Speaking is something I love to do. I'm glad it shows."

He takes his left hand to cup it over the two of our hands still embraced in our handshake and says, "You need to share your story. You need to share your other story, the story you received assistance from my staff. You can help our military servicemen and women. We need you. May I have one of my staff connect with you to discuss how we can set this up?"

A bell rings in my head. It's sort of a deja vu of words that were said to me two years earlier by Tom, the veterans' service officer. It was Tom's initial statement that prompted me to re-open my VA claim. It was Tom who said, "Thank you for your service. I believe you have a voice to help others who can't speak for themselves." Our congressman has just asked me to share my story to help others. His request moves me, and I agree to meet with his staff. I know it can take time to set up these types of engagements, so I'll wait patiently. In the meantime, Tom has asked me to testify to the California State Senate Committee on Veterans Affairs. The necessary budget to support the Veterans Service Offices across the state is up for review. My testimony and presentation about my experience in the Air Force and how the local office assisted me in obtaining benefits will secure the vote. The audience of senators is much smaller than the theaters of people I've inspired and trained in the past, but the topic I'm going to be presenting feels much bigger. Cameras are mounted on the wall to my left and right, but it's who is behind me that can see me most clearly. It's Aidar who's sitting in the audience and recording my speech. He's holding up a cell phone and, more importantly, is how he holds my heart. He knows the power with which I'm speaking. Aidar stands with me as we pull off the blanket that has covered these atrocities, and I confidently testify to the events. It's Aidar who has helped me build strong walls to withstand the difficult years. I may be the one who's speaking, but it's his strength and encouragement that holds me strong. To testify in this forum is as much of a celebration for him as it is for me. One of the senators wipes the tears from his eyes as I tell of my experience, but it's the sobs I hear from many people in the room that motivate me to continue speaking. My voice is shaking. With every tear rolling down my cheek, I privately scream, *"You won't silence me ever again."*

Annamarie testifies to California State
Senate in Sacramento, CA

More and more healing is showering over me; I've been asked to participate in a program at Travis Air Force base. This program stems from an introduction provided to me by the staff of our congressman. I'm not surprised he followed through with his suggestion. The congressman has reinforced my faith in people, especially men in politics. The program is called

Military Storytellers, and it allows military personnel to share a life experience or challenge with other military personnel. It has been my dream to share my story with others and encourage them in many different ways. I'm hopeful the Sexual Assault Response Program now implemented across the military will decrease the incidence of rape and encourage those who may be victims, seek counseling, and fight their attacker. My years as an accomplished speaker aren't helping me to deal with some of the emotions I'm feeling right now. Standing before several thousand Air Force personnel to share my experience is thrilling but frightening. I'm not at all frightened or concerned about the number of people in the audience. I have no fear that I won't move my audience or lose them in a message I was trying to convey. I know that everyone will learn something they'll immediately be able to apply to their lives. I'm concerned I might rip open an old emotional wound within myself, and hemorrhage in the days following the series.

The program is scheduled on the base for two weeks, three times each week. I'm excited and incredibly honored. I receive a notice from the director of the Storytellers speaker series asking me to attend a meeting with the other eight speakers. In addition to me, there will be five other men and three women. Each speaker has a different subject and story to share. This first meeting of all of the speakers is riddled with surprises. We meet in a small room and sit in a circle on cold, metal folding chairs. The other speakers are more than thirty-five years younger than me, and they're all still active in the military. Their formal vocabulary and the way they're so quick to refer to me as "Ma'am" is a reminder of both my age and the fact I'm not part of the currently enlisted club. Their uniforms are crisp, clean, and they segregate me from the pack.

The discrepancy of age and profession dissipates as we each give a quick overview of the life challenges we'll share with the audience. There are four men and four women who bravely reveal personal stories that strip us of our protective shells. Challenges with spousal abuse, alcohol dependence, and depression overlap with death experiences, battlefield scars, and PTSD. Each of us has come to this meeting to give a brief overview of what we intend to share when we're on stage. We all intend to share our stories to help others. We want to encourage our audience to be strong, courageous, and convicted in their success with overcoming their challenges. My eyes fill up with tears as each person shares their personal stories of struggle and triumph. In my mind, each of the young women scheduled to speak looks like me when I was their age. Regardless of their ethnicity, stature, or even the story they tell, I see myself. I want to leave the room. I want to take every one of these young girls home with me. Each one of them is a woman, grown and fully independent. However, my inner voice is screaming at me, *"Annamarie, get all of these young girls out of here and put them in your car."* It takes every ounce of restraint to not scream at them to *"Come on; you're leaving with me. I'll keep you safe."* The moment we exit the meeting room, I feel better.

Across the parking lot and quite a ways away, I see the beautiful young Airman who shared her battle with depression. I shout out to her, "Excuse me. May I talk with you for a moment?"

Her car keys are dangling from her fingers. Tears are running down her face, and I'm concerned. "Are you alright?" I ask.

"I'm fine." She replies. "It's just the emotion of sharing the story that has me a little melancholy."

"It's perfectly natural, honey. I'm old enough to be your mother, maybe even your grandmother. You can tell me it's none of my business; but, are you okay? I mean, are you safe? Are you okay with going home? Okay, to go to work? Anything--are you okay? If you're not okay, you can come home with me."

I stop talking. I think this young Airman may think I'm a little crazy. She wipes the tears from her eyes and begins to smile and says, "Wow. That makes me happy to know you care."

It's the sincerity of her smile that brings me back to reality, and I recognize that I can't kidnap every female on the base home.

More importantly, I realize that I don't need to bring them home to protect them. I know that if I bring several young Airmen home with me, Aidar will think that I've mentally "lost it." I just want her to know I care. I know I was able to get that point across.

Before climbing into our cars to leave, she hugs me and assures me she truly is okay. It's a passion of mine always to make others know there's someone who cares. It's especially important to me for people to understand how to care enough about themselves. When she drives away, I sit in my car and cry. Now that I know more about PTSD, I can observe some of my behaviors and deal with them rationally; without judgment. I believe we're all just hoping someone will "care." Other than my family and very close friends, I never felt my rape mattered to anyone. I know the system didn't "care" about me. I believe the system cared more about suppressing my rape than it ever did about "me."

At the age of nineteen and in the fragile state of mind I was in following my rape, I wasn't able to care for myself. I needed help. I wasn't in a position to fight by myself. I was in no condition to pursue exposing the truth. For the last thirty-eight years, I've crafted a career around teaching others how to overcome the obstacles that are keeping them from their dreams and goals. I've designed a life teaching others how to overcome the one thing I had not. Until now! Every day I speak with the Military Storyteller's Program, I hear gasps out in the audience as they are filled with outrage. While I look out into the hundreds of people in the crowd, I see my young face. I make sure to let them know that I care, and I provide them with the names of agencies available to them if they need assistance and support. Programs are in place to help with the challenges they're facing and ever will face in life. Not all of the agencies are in the military system. Many agencies are private.

Sharing the truths of my experience gives me power. It's only by helping others that I'm able to fill the hollow in my spirit. I have the power and ability to direct my life; I am not a victim. I am a conqueror.

Annamarie speaks at Storytellers, Travis AFB, CA

CHAPTER 5

★ ★ ★ ★ ★

Evolution

I am reminded every day that a caterpillar really can learn to fly, but only if it wants to. Evolving from the caterpillar is a struggle. It's painful to push through the cocoon and exercise our wings. I really do love to fly.

The "One Size Fits All" counseling I received on my dime, never addressed the specific needs of a woman who experienced the violence of rape. I was only nineteen; the coping mechanisms I created for myself proved to be more damaging than helpful. With no support from the military, I had to become a counselor and develop my tools to merely survive. Abraham Lincoln, who was a lawyer himself, had a quote that hits home for me now. He said, "He who represents himself has a fool for a client." While trying to cope and counsel myself over the years, I've come to recognize I lack the proper "know-how" to treat the effects of PTSD. I'm beginning to feel foolish.

Anger and resentment have become familiar tastes in my mouth, yet I mask them in various artificial flavors and behaviors. Despite my upbringing in Christianity, which taught me we'll all be judged when we die, I've been holding on to a silent wish for the man who raped me. I've been holding on tightly to a quiet desire for revenge; it's etching a groove on my soul while it plays over and over. I don't want my rapist to wait until the day he dies to seek forgiveness. I privately hope he will feel pain and suffer while he's here and alive on earth. I want him to know what it feels like to hurt and feel the pain when someone in his family is in pain or broken. I have a secret wish for his wife, mother, sister, or daughter to suffer pain. I know this is an awful belief; I'm not proud of my thoughts. I admit I feel ashamed of my feelings; I know they're not good.

I remind myself of the story about a woman and her Easter ham. In this story, a woman is asked, "How do you prepare your Easter ham?" The woman said, "I cut off both ends of the ham, pack the top with pineapple and cloves and cook it until it reaches the internal temperature of 145'." The woman is then asked, "Why do you cut off both ends of the ham?" She replied, "That's the way my mother use to cook it." They reached out to the Grandmother and asked her, "Why do you cut off both ends of your ham before you cook it?" The Grandmother said, "That's the way my mother cooked it." Moving up one more generation, the Great-Grandmother was asked why she cuts the ends off the ham, and she replied, "Because the ham wouldn't fit in my pan." For the past forty years, I've used only one way to cope with my rape memories. I've told myself to be grateful you're alive. I've been trying to apply this one way of thinking to all the different situations. I force myself to look at the "benefit" of all problems, including tragedy. Like the woman who only follows one recipe and cooks the ham in the same old manner, I've not allowed myself to grow. Just as I have changed over the years, my coping skills also need to change. The old recipe I've been using to appease the fact my rapist was never even pursued by the military police, let alone apprehended, has served me well. The only reason why this one technique has worked is that I've never learned anything new.

Θ　　Θ　　Θ

Business travel isn't as glamorous as it looks. As a professional speaker, I've paid a high price for traveling and working on the road. It has cost me a great deal in the area of friendships. I have friends around the globe, but not many friends close to my own home. Last week I attended a local women's club meeting where I met a woman with a personality similar to my own; we just clicked. We've decided to meet this afternoon for lunch. I want to get to know her and hopefully develop a friendship.

Bubbling over with enthusiasm, I feel like a human glass of champagne. I'm looking forward to learning all about her life and sharing some part of myself that I rarely have the opportunity to reveal. Scarlett is a beautiful woman. She's captivating and impeccably groomed. Her blue eyes sparkle bright when she smiles. Everything from her hair, clothes, accessories, and make-up are placed with great intention on her body. This attention to detail presents an image of a woman who has great pride in herself; I'm impressed. I like to look my best; however, I generally throw on my lipstick without a mirror's assistance. If I do use a mirror, it's usually the rear-view mirror in my car. Scarlett has lined her lips with great detail; her lipstick beautifully complements her outfit and is glossed exquisitely.

The moment we settle into our seats in the restaurant, I quickly lead off with a question. "You go first," I say. "Tell me all about yourself; where were you born?"

Without hesitation, Scarlett begins to share her life story. Jumping in now and then with a question or comment, I'm amazed by how much we have in common. We both have professional careers, we're married, and each of us only has one child; a son. Here's my chance to find a commonality we can discuss.

"You say you have a son?" I ask. Where does he live?"

I'm sure I've misunderstood her answer to my question, so I ask it again.

"I'm sorry, where did you say he lives?"

Her voice is hesitant. I listen more closely to her when she says, "I don't usually share this with everyone, but I feel comfortable with you; I feel safe."

"That's nice to hear. Please, go on."

"My son is in San Quentin prison. He was accused and sentenced for the rape of a woman," she says.

I hear her voice; I see her lips moving, but the loud crumbling noise from the destruction and collapse of my coping skills is most distracting. In an earthquake, I'd quickly run to stand under a doorframe, but there's no place to run in my psyche. In my head, there are no tables where I can crawl and hide. I could always retreat to the safe place in my thoughts and avoid the subject altogether; but, I don't want to. I don't want to hide from myself. I want to stay in the light and focus on what I'm feeling. I want to use my newly found coping skills to remain present, so I can continue to learn. I want to know about *"me."* I'm aware of my discomfort with the situation; I'm uncomfortable in my skin, but I'm going to stay with this moment. All of my senses are running on high.

The texture of the white linen napkin draped across my lap has all of my attention. If I rub this napkin any harder between my thumb and fingertips, I'm going to make a hole. The droplets of water trickling down the outside of my water glass distract me. My focus diverts to the feeling I have pulling at my heart; it's tearing at the logical part of my brain. My shoulders tense up. I'd love to shrink down and sink into one of the single drops of water moving slowly from the rim of the water glass to the stem. I'm not positive if I'm swimming in this drop of water and still in control of my emotions or if I'm about to be out of control and drowning. I widen my gaze to look away from the glass and take in all of Scarlett. As I watch the tears pour from her eyes, my entire body becomes flush. I feel the blood drain from my face. I don't need a mirror to know I look pasty white. Sweat covers my forehead, and I feel nauseous.

As Scarlet shares her pain and heartache, the jagged-edged grooves etched into my behavior from years of misdirected coping skills are softening. Like me, it's clear she's suffered at the hands of another. I could never wish her harm; yet, this is what I've been doing for over three decades. Just as generations of women continue to cut the end pieces off the Easter ham because that was how their mothers taught them, I have relied on an outdated method of coping.

For only a brief moment, I pause to apply one of the new techniques I've learned to ground myself. I want to stay present and control my reaction. I slowly take in my breath and hold it and slowly exhale. I use my other tool to engage my senses. It only takes me a moment to use the "5, 4, 3, 2, 1 exercise." I identify five objects, four different sounds, three textures, two smells, and one taste. I bring my attention to the present.

It's with an incredible force that our two worlds collide. The taste I've identified to ground myself is coming from a large piece of sourdough bread. This lump of bread sits in a ball at the back of my throat. I'm mesmerized and motionless, but I'm not anxious or feeling overwhelmed. Right now, the only thing I'm trying to digest is the significance of our meeting. It's taking all my restraint not to look to God, throw my hands up to the sky and say, "Are you kidding me right now? This isn't funny." Without knowing my story, I'm sure she's confused by my actions. It doesn't matter if someone is in physical or emotional pain; I have an overwhelming desire to comfort her. Instinctively, my heart takes the lead. I'll comfort her. I reach across the table to touch her arm, but I'm stopped in my tracks when she says, "It bothers me so many women falsely claim rape. It sickens me."

Pulling my hand back quickly, it looks as if I just touched a burning hot skillet. My instinct tempts me to fall back on an old belief, an outdated coping skill. Thank goodness the emotions of my heart speak louder than the revengeful thoughts tucked away in my mind. I know that if I shut down, I'll close myself off from a great woman and a new friendship. If I carefully open up to her right now, I might be able to use this opportunity to heal two hearts with one gesture. With one deep breath, I fill myself up with courage and share my story with Scarlet. Rivers of tears pour from my eyes. Scarlet's mouth drops in shock. I was right to presume that she and I are similar in our personalities. While I sit here and share my story, she evaluates her assumptions and shares her insights along with our conversation.

Lunch ends on a super high note; we walk away forever changed women. Scarlet and I have established a bond built upon the shattering of beliefs and outdated points of view. I feel liberated by the shattering of a misaligned coping skill that no longer served me.

I have great compassion and understanding for the nineteen-year-old girl who lives inside me. I accept that my private bitterness "was" a coping skill I needed at that time to survive. I have no judgment of myself for the thoughts and feelings I privately held. This thinking, no matter how harsh, has helped me over the years to survive. I was doing the best I could to make it through a day.

From a very young age, we're conditioned and programmed to conform and follow a "set format" of behaviors. When I'm speaking on this specific topic, I enjoy watching my audience's faces when I demonstrate this conditioning. I ask everyone to stand up and touch their toes. Giggling, I watch as hundreds of people struggle to bend over and reach for their toes. Frequently, they look around the room to see how far others can stretch. I continue talking about the difference of what happens when I give these same instructions to children, specifically children who haven't had a formal gym class. Young children, around the age of four or five, don't bend over at the waist to touch their toes. Instead, children come up with all sorts of creative alternative methods to reach their feet. Kids will bring their toes up to their hands in the front of them or flipping their feet from the back; children are creative. Once we attend a structured gym class, we learn that the "proper" way to touch our toes is to bend over at the waist. It's moments like these where our creativity gets lost. Throughout our life, society tells us the appropriate ways to behave, react, and respond to emotions and humanity. Habits are established, and frequently our creativity is washed away.

Change can be painful and uncomfortable, and we will often grieve the person we once were or the innocence we lost. It takes time to adapt to change, just as it takes time to grieve. Processes like this can't be rushed. Grieving is painful, but I teach my audience that if you try to eliminate the pain associated with change, you'll never grow. To demonstrate my point, I use a toy cloth caterpillar. To me, one of the best examples of change is a caterpillar. A caterpillar moves along the ground and crawls on a plant munching leaves. When it's time to change, it will attach itself to a twig and spin around and shed its skin to become a chrysalis. Inside here is where the work is done, and when completed, it struggles to change. Children regularly take a mason jar and poke holes in the lid for air. They place a caterpillar on a stick with some leaves and wait to watch this transformation. Upon watching the butterfly struggle to break out, they frequently use their tiny fingers to open the hard shell to help the butterfly emerge. When they take the struggle away from the butterfly, it can't fly. You see, it's the process of the struggle that allows the butterfly to gain strength in its wings and fly. While on stage, my toy caterpillar opens up to reveal the beautiful wings full of color and design. True metamorphosis! The struggle we have through grieving reveals us. It exposes our new self. It reveals who we are without someone. The next step is to accept who we are in our new form. To the caterpillar, these new beautiful wings feel strange; until it learns to move them and fly. The butterfly may grieve the loss of the caterpillar until it opens its eyes and enjoys the view from above.

EPILOGUE

The journey of *"Hollowed Soldier: Raped in the Military and Abandoned,"* began with the rape and hollowing of my spirit on October 5ᵗʰ, 1977. In my first book, *"Hollowed" An Amazing True Story of a Woman Who Endured the Hollowing of Her Spirit, Body and Soul,* my soul was hollowed when Austin passed on October 5ᵗʰ, 2018. No, that isn't a typo; it's just a cruel irony. When I began writing, Austin was alive and cheering me on. When Austin passed away, I had no desire to finish the book; I was in a total mental fog. However, at the Celebration of Life service that we held for him, I found many silver linings in a very dark cloud. One of these joys was reconnecting family members I hadn't seen in years. One, in particular, is our niece Kim McCoy. Similar to how Austin encouraged me, Kim urged me to pick up the book and continue. It wasn't until she was reading the chapter on the rape that she noticed the date. Kim asked me if there was a mistake in the date of my rape documented in the hospital intake report. When she reminded me that October 5ᵗʰ was the date of my spiritual hollowing and soulful hollowing, I was speechless.

The young girl in 1977 is still in my heart. The character traits instilled in me while growing up are strong and have only grown with me. With the incredible support and partnership of Aidar and Austin, I was able to focus my determination to take on the

VA. I know I'll never be able to hold the rapist accountable, but having the VA acknowledge their error helps me heal. Instead of spewing my anger of the Air Force and VA out into the air with no results, I'm able to be productive and help other military personnel. I'm able to fill my hollowed spirit by giving to other military personnel the tools to communicate more effectively to prevent harassment, assault, and wrongful discharge. It's also healing to be able to help others to heal their spirit when wronged or damaged.

The VA granted me benefits for the appeal I filed in 2013 for the decision they made in error in 1978. I received medical benefits and assistance for the MST and PTSD I suffered from the rape and back injury. The new appeal I filed in 2014 is for the correction to the verbiage they used to claim I had a "character of behavior" disorder since birth has yet to be heard by the judge. I have waited over forty years to have my day in court finally; another two won't hurt.

It's my dream to have my book, *"Hollowed Soldier,"* open a door even wider to share my story to help others. The US Military and Veterans Administration are two of the largest giants in America. We must hold the perpetrators accountable. I am disheartened to read in the Statistics from the 2016 – 2020 Dod SAPRO Reports and their appendices; Updated May 2020, that sexual violence remains pervasive. In FY 18, 20,500 service members were sexually assaulted or raped, including 13,000 women and 7,500 men. The rate of sexual assault and rape jumped by almost 40% from FY 16 to FY 18, and for women the rate increased by over 50% to the highest level since 2006. Of women who reported penetrative sexual assault, 59% were assaulted by someone with a higher rank than them, and 24% were assaulted by someone in their chain of command. 76.1% of victims did not report the crime in FY 18. A third of the victims are discharged after reporting, typically within seven months of making a report. Victims receiving harsher discharges, with 24% separated under less than fully honorable conditions, compared to 15% of all service members.

The prevalence of rape, harassment, retaliation, and wrongful discharge of the victims in the military reached epidemic levels many years ago. The lack of prosecution of the perpetrators has created an environment that degrades and devalues the greatness we know lies in the hearts of the majority of our good servicemen and women. This culture of violence must be reformed in order for our military to be truly the best.

Through writing, I've rediscovered that I'm forever growing and learning, as the alternative is certain death. I learn from every living thing around me, including the birds and the trees. I will never speak from a platform of, "Do as I say, not as I do." I plan to continue on my path and learn from you as we connect.

Forty years of my life was required to gather the material in this book and my previous book, "*Hollowed.*" Once the truth began to flow from my heart and onto the keys of my computer, I couldn't stop. As a professional speaker, trainer, and comedienne, I found my identity in the words I speak and not the words I write. It's been easy for me to stand up before three-thousand people and give an off-the-cuff speech that moves them to an arousing standing ovation. On the other hand, I've discovered that writing is a beautiful way to stretch, grow, and finish what trauma and grief brought upon me.

Donna VanLiere writes, "Grief never ends.....but it changes. It's a passage, not a place to stay. Grief is not a sign of weakness nor a lack of faith. It is the price of love."

I grieve the person I was before the rape. I lost the trusting young woman who had faith in others and institutions. Obviously, I needed to have my naivety removed but not yanked and cut out of me through the violence of rape. Although my spirit was hollowed, my attacker left with nothing I couldn't put back together. He didn't hold my spirit in his hands, yet it was missing when he walked out the door of my barracks. My effervescent young self struggled to trust. I struggled to trust others, but more importantly, I struggled to trust myself. I was only able to fill this hollow place in my spirit by helping others and taking risks with my giving. With the large hole, I had more room within my heart to hold and help more people. Administering compassion and support to other young women in a similar circumstance, I provided an example for them to emulate. This behavior demonstrated my ability to regain strength and trust. This outreach once again made my spirit healthy and full. The legal system has deadlines for filing required documents to prosecute the attacker or seek retribution. Often these requirements can't be met, and we're not always able to rectify some misdeeds, but it's never too late to confront the demons inside of us and heal our emotional wounds. Demonstrating love for others is precisely how you begin to fill a hollowed spirit.

While filling my spirit with empathy and love for others, I am empowered. It's been a beautiful struggle to expand myself from a speaker into a writer. To have helped at least one person with their life allows me to fly and ride the wind's waves.

Hollowed Soldier
Raped in the Military and Abandoned

ACKNOWLEDGMENTS

I may be the puzzle, but you and everyone I meet are my pieces.

Θ   Θ   Θ

There are three people; I call them my special angels, who made this entire book possible. Two of them are angels here on earth, and the other now has wings. They are my husband, Aidar, our son Austin, and our niece Kim McCoy.

My first word of thanks and gratitude goes to Aidar. While standing in the bank line in 1979, who would have known we would travel on such a fantastic journey together. He is my friend, husband, partner, and my strength. Any accolades for this book belong to him. I like to refer to him as my breath, my spirit protector. The unwavering faith he has in me keeps me moving. His gentle nudging to press on and finish writing Hollowed and Hollowed Soldier picked me up and pushed me forward when I was without focus. He gave clarity to my dream. Without him, I wouldn't have the courage to share my story, our story. I'm in awe of his love and support as he is the cornerstone of the strength I needed to confront the US Military and Veteran Administration. Together, we'll stand firm, grow wildly, and always live in the

Three Musketeers' spirit. I count my blessings every day to have him in my life.

The second magical being is our son Austin. He left his earthly body and spread his heavenly wings too soon; he is now my spirit angel. When he left, my soul was hollowed. I am so proud to forever be called Austin's mom. He was, and he continues to be my muse and writing partner. His beautiful touch and positive influence on earth continue to ripple through all the lives he touched. I miss him dearly and will continue to "Live Big and Be Happy" because of him. Austin is the one person I must thank for continually reminding me for whom I wrote this book. I will always treasure his encouragement to transition from a speaker to a writer.

The third magical being is our niece Kim McCoy. Her love and influence came when one of the more massive waves of grief was toppling over me. The effervescence of her character pulled me up and pointed me back in the right direction. Without her dedication to reading, editing, and supporting my writing, I was lost. Without her, this book would be locked away and left to gather dust.

I've never walked alone in this world. At every turn on the road to publishing, my friends and family have shown me love, support, and encouragement. I want to thank all of them for walking with me and for their unwavering support.

I want to give my brother Peder a special note of thanks for challenging me always to be true to myself. Our long and sincere conversations gave me inspiration and motivation.

I'm incredibly grateful to my very first friend in life. Eileen Emerson and I were friends while we were still in our mothers' wombs. Her constant push on me to finish the book was both the carrot and the stick. Knowing she is always near, no matter how far apart we may live, is something I value and will forever treasure.

Thank you to all my clients in Title & Escrow, Real Estate, and all the ancillary companies as well as all the military installations and cancer treatment centers. Your influence supports every word in this book, and your support fuels me today and always.

I want to acknowledge the influences of joy and sadness. I'm grateful to have both of them in my life. To have one of them without the other would limit my appreciation of true happiness. Without sadness, I'd never fully appreciated the power of joy and the pleasure of sharing it. Without the discomfort of sadness, I'd never be motivated and inspired to break out of its grasp. This inspiration pushed me to take the necessary steps to work through the pain and return to joy. Their influence makes it possible to share with others the tools to move through life with greater appreciation. They have taught me greater empathy, understanding, and love.

I want to thank you, my reader. I value the time you've dedicated to reading this story. When you find yourself hollowed, give more. The most everlasting way to fill yourself back up is with love, light, and laughter by giving to others.

CPSIA information can be obtained
at www.ICGtesting.com
Printed in the USA
LVHW050004041120
670570LV00003B/235